THE
MAKING OF AMERICA
SERIES

WESTERN SISKIYOU COUNTY

GOLD AND DREAMS

CHAMPS OF SISKIYOU, 1920. The Fort Jones High School basketball players pictured here are, from left to right, (front row) J. Branson, Captain G. McBride, D. Mathews, and P. Evans; (back row) I. Luce, Coach Roy Sharp, F. Reichman, and H. Piscantor. (Courtesy Betty Hall–Irene Nelson Collection.)

FRONT COVER: *Two miners pose with their diggings in the Black Bear Mine Area (Courtesy Siskiyou County Museum.)*

THE
MAKING OF AMERICA
SERIES

WESTERN SISKIYOU COUNTY
GOLD AND DREAMS

GAIL L. FIORINI-JENNER AND
MONICA JAE HALL

ARCADIA

Published by Arcadia Publishing
Charleston SC, Chicago IL, Portsmouth NH, San Francisco CA

First published 2002.
Reprinted 2005.

Library of Congress Catalog Card Number: 2002108721

For all general information contact Arcadia Publishing at:
Telephone 843-853-2070
Fax 843-853-0044
E-Mail sales@arcadiapublishing.com
For customer service and orders:
Toll-Free 1-888-313-2665

Visit us on the Internet at www.arcadiapublishing.com

CONTENTS

ACKNOWLEDGMENTS

Wallace Stegner wrote, in the foreword of *The Big Sky* by A.B. Guthrie, "History is an artifact. It does not exist until it is remembered and written down; and it is not truly remembered or written down until it has been vividly imagined. We become our past, and it becomes a part of us, by the reliving of our beginnings."

So it is with this volume; as we endeavored to gather as much into this narrow space as possible, we let our cumulative imagination direct our writing. There could be volumes added to this single one, full of the stories we had to tuck into folders for some future time, but we are indebted to all those who enthusiastically shared their family or community histories. Each story took on a life of its own. For all those we interviewed, we wish we could have included every precious memory or photograph. We hope you will not be disappointed with the final results. In addition, we have worked to remain as faithful and accountable to history as possible. A very special thanks and tribute is given to Jeff Buchin, without whose assistance and patience we would have struggled and missed every deadline. His expertise was invaluable.

Special thanks are also extended to the following societies and individuals for their invaluable contributions to this volume: Siskiyou County Historical Society and Museum; Bernita Tickner; Betty Jane Young; Betty and Roy Hall Sr. and Roy Hall Jr.; Charlie and Pam Hayden; Dick Luttrell; Homer Barandun; Bill Balfrey; Katie Berthelson; Mary Sovey; Liz Dillman-Bowen; Jeanie Griggs and the McBroom family; Harold and MaryLou Slette; Jack and GloryAnn Jenner; Bob and Alisa (Hiett) Brown; Bernard and Bev Dowling; Nell and Pinky Bill Mathews; Dorothy Hayden; Nancy Hayden; Shelley Starr and the Starr family; Sara Whipple; Brian Helsaple; Mike Hendryx; Mike and Lynne Bryan; Cecilia Reuter and the Fort Jones Museum; Trinity County Historical Society; Ginny Laustalot; Curtis (Tuffy) Fowler; Rod Eastlick; Ellen Hayden; Buzz Helm; Carolyn Pimentel; Chet McBroom; Jim Rock; Steve and Martha Lindgren; Jan Baker; Karen (Short) Kraus; Jasha Reynolds; Greg Lindholm; Debbie Levulett; Margie (Shelton) Genter; Janet Muzinich; Jim Falkawski; Hal Hewes for his computer help; and everyone else who gave us either inspiration or information.

A final thanks goes to our husbands, Doug Jenner and Roy Hall Jr., and our children, who put up with our frantic schedule and crazy hours.

INTRODUCTION

Nestled between the mountains separating the Sacramento Valley and the Oregon border rests the vast region of Siskiyou County. Five times larger than the state of Rhode Island, it is the fifth largest county in land size in California, but one of the least populated and least understood. So vast and diverse, Siskiyou County's rich history must be divided into separate geographic regions, thus *Western Siskiyou County: Gold and Dreams* represents the story of less than one-third of its population. And it must be added that this small volume cannot do justice to the individuals who pioneered this county, Native American, immigrant, or settler.

From pre-contact days, when the Shasta and Karuk tribes inhabited the region without conflict or interruption, to the present, people have been drawn to Western Siskiyou County for a variety of reasons. Sheltered river canyons dip to 500 feet above sea level while rugged snow-capped ridges rise to 8,000 feet and beyond. Half hidden within these ranges are small narrow valleys. For 150 years, these mountains, rivers, and valleys have provided refuge and resources to early miners and pioneers, and their descendants.

The region presently encompasses 2,900 square miles and includes the Klamath National Forest, the Marble Mountain Wilderness-Primitive Area (home of over 200 glacier lakes), and the Trinity-Salmon Alps. The Klamath River, the third largest in California, rises up out of the Klamath Lakes, then moves westerly towards the ocean. As it surges on, several other wild rivers pour into it, including the Shasta, Salmon, Scott, and Trinity. The volume of water flowing through the mountainous, rocky gorges explains why the Native Americans called it the "Swift" river.

In 1873, Siskiyou County was the largest county in northern California, extending from Del Norte County in the west across to the Nevada state line, nearly 200 miles east to west. From north to south, it extended 60 miles. It encompassed 5.5 million acres, including 1 million acres of forests and 500,000 acres of lakes, and was as large as Rhode Island, Delaware, and Massachusetts combined. A rich mining region as well, its steep river gorges and basins were traversed by miners—on foot or with pack trains—in their quest to strike it rich.

In 1874, Klamath County was dissolved and divided between Humboldt and Siskiyou Counties, while the eastern portion of Siskiyou County was taken away and annexed to the newly created Modoc County. In 1887, the area held by Del Norte County along the upper Klamath River became part of Siskiyou County. But it wasn't until 1901 that the formal boundaries delineating Siskiyou County, as we know it today, were legislated.

Tucked away between the mountain ranges lay three major valleys that have contributed substantially to the area's agricultural and economic base since the 1850s: Scott Valley, Quartz Valley, and Seiad Valley. The communities and towns located within these regions include Callahan (pop. 175), Cecilville, Etna (pop. 760), Forks of Salmon, Fort Jones (pop. 640), Fort Goff, Greenview (pop. 150), Hamburg, Happy Camp (700), Klamath River, Horse Creek, Scott Bar, Seiad, and Somes Bar. The remaining areas are unincorporated, but are home to approximately 8,000 people. Historically, of course, this land was home to thousands more.

Russian fur trappers possibly entered the region as early as 1825, and Jedediah Smith reportedly crossed through the Trinity Mountains above the mouth of the Klamath River in 1828. But it was the Hudson Bay trappers Stephen Meek, Thomas McKay, George Aldophus Duzel, and 16 other men, along with a number of horses, who discovered the area called Beaver Valley in 1836 (now called Scott Valley). Meek later declared that Scott Valley had been one of the best places to trap beaver and wild game and, though he went on to hunt and trap all over the West, he returned to the Josiah Doll ranch in Scott Valley in 1871. Here he lived until his death in 1889 at the age of 90. He was buried in the Etna Cemetery. Today, there are still a number of "potholes" near Oro Fino that are supposedly remnants from the days when trappers dug out great fire pits, and until a few years ago, the remains of a two-story "sod house" could be found where the Etna Union High School football field is now. According to Bill Balfrey, whose grandmother knew its original history, the structure had been an early "fort" for the Hudson Bay trappers.

As with the rest of California, it was the great Gold Rush of 1849 that opened the doors to Siskiyou County. Harry L. Wells, in *History of Siskiyou County, California*, credits the first mining in this region to Lindsay Applegate, who traveled south from Jacksonville, Oregon in 1849 to mine along Beaver Creek, the Klamath, and the Scott River. In June of 1850, however, prospectors from the Trinity River crossed the Salmon-Trinity Alps and found enough gold to whet their appetites. John W. Scott, from whom the valley and river later derived their names, discovered gold at "Scott's Bar."

Within a year, the "northern mines" were drawing prospectors from every part of the world—perhaps as many as 20,000—who, "like coveys of scared quail, scuttled hither and thither." Without roads, the only manner of travel was by foot or mule train. Few stayed in one place long, though settlements throughout the region boasted booming populations at various times. Hamburg, for instance, a tiny spot on today's map, swelled to a population of about 5,000. Somes Bar, at the junction of the Klamath and Salmon Rivers, listed 500 to 1,000 men in 1852, though by 1908, the area had little more than a store and hotel. Deadwood, a settlement established at the forks of Deadwood and Cherry Creeks, grew to such prominence that it vied for county seat. Yreka, today's county seat, won its title by only two votes, while Deadwood no longer exists, except in the memories of a few old-timers.

Most of the miners eventually left for other regions after the gold petered out, or died penniless and destitute, even nameless. Others settled in the valleys and along the rivers' edges, some to turn their hand to logging or ranching or to take up mining in a limited way. These are the industries that have sustained Western Siskiyou County for five generations.

Only in the last three decades has a new wave of settlers moved across this green and gold landscape, those hoping to escape the fast-paced world of city living. As a result, communities once thought to be isolated and insulated from outside forces are becoming more and more linked to the bigger world.

It is our hope that this book can reach out to that larger world and offer up a tiny insight into this marvelous, majestic region. *Western Siskiyou County: Gold and Dreams* is dedicated to all those who have lived, worked, and died here, as well as to those who now make it their home.

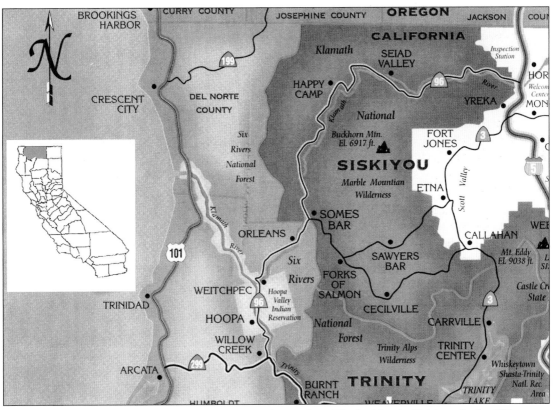

MAP OF SISKIYOU COUNTY. *Five times larger than Rhode Island, Siskiyou is the fifth largest county in California, but one of the least populated and most diverse.*

1. THE FIRST PEOPLE AND EARLY CONTACT

Western Siskiyou County is a land of constantly changing seasons, people, and landscape. Originally, Western Siskiyou was home to two aboriginal tribes, the Kutekekanac (Shasta) and the Quoratem (Karuk). Because the names of the various tribes have been recorded with so many alternative spellings, the current tribal names and spellings are used for some simplification and clarity.

The Shasta occupied most of what is now Siskiyou County, south into Shasta County, and north into southern Oregon, an area approximately 200 miles wide and 200 miles long with almost 20 million acres. Scott Valley, Salmon River, down to the Wooley Creek drainage, and the Klamath River, north of Scott Valley, denote Western Siskiyou County—Shasta aboriginal lands that are covered in this text.

When the first Hudson Bay trappers arrived in the region during the 1830s, they not only found rivers and lakes filled with beaver, otter, and mink, but also the 14,500-foot mountain that towered over the broad valley (now known as Shasta Valley). They were so impressed that they named the mountain, the valley surrounding it, and the natives who inhabited it "Sasté." The names were eventually changed to Mount Shasta, Shasta Valley, and the Shasta Tribe. The translation for the Russian word *sasté* is "pure and white."

After the Russian fur trappers left their mark, the chief who lived near the mountain became known as Shastika. The name Shasta was more pronounceable than Kutekekanac and, within a span of a few generations, only oral native family histories recalled the original name of the people.

The Shasta numbered in the thousands prior to European contact and their diseases. Tall and lean with lighter skin than most northwest peoples, some Shasta even had red hair. Their refined features and distinctly different structure of tribal life set them apart from their neighboring tribes. There is no migration story. It is said that "Waka [God] stepped down from the heavens onto the top of the mountain [Mount Shasta] and placed the people around the mountain. Here they flourished."

The Shasta government was orderly and strict. The tribe was physically divided by the towering mountains and various valleys in the region. There was one chief,

SALMON RIVER COUNTRY. The Salmon is one of the last wild rivers in California. (Courtesy Siskiyou County Museum.)

Sky, over all the Shasta when the fur trappers arrived. His sons were the leaders of each of the eight bands of Shasta. There were several sub-chiefs and lesser chiefs, who helped maintain a secure life by administering swift justice to those who violated the laws.

Of the eight bands of Shasta, four lived in the western Siskiyou area: the Scott Valley; the Konomehu, in the Salmon River area; the New River, further west and south of the Konomehu; and the Upper Klamath, along the Klamath River north of Scott Valley. A family member was allowed to marry into a family in a different band no closer than every eight generations, which kept the people from marrying close relatives and kept social and political ties strong.

The Grand Conclave was an annual gathering of chiefs and select tribal members from the western tribes. It was held further east every few years. It was similar to a harvest festival where foodstuffs, trade goods, and tribal information were exchanged. At the Grand Conclave, the Shasta's marriage wheel was further used to build strong ties to tribes both far and near. Marriages were arranged throughout the western states. These ties between tribes made travel safe for all.

Since adultery was taken as a serious offense, an adulterous man was killed and the woman was thrown on a burning brush pile. Violent or criminal activities were punished by sending perpetrators to the furthest reaches of eastern Siskiyou

MRS. EFFMAN, HAPPY CAMP 1912. Woven of willow, bear grass, pine root, and maidenhair fern, baskets were a vital part of Shasta and Karuk material culture. (Courtesy Fort Jones Museum.)

County (land of the Modoc tribes), a land of swamps and lava beds. With such harsh punishments, there was little crime or unacceptable behavior.

Living in permanent villages and traveling to gathering areas, the Shasta depended on the seasons and harvest. In the spring, the Shasta gathered *icknish*, also known as wild celery. *Icknish* was used for food and ceremonial purposes. *Epohs* were one of the mainstays of the Shasta diet and it took the whole tribe to dig up enough of the pea-sized, potato-like vegetable to last the people through the long winters. Other foods gathered during the spring, summer, and fall were acorns, pine nuts, and berries. They ripened earlier in the lower valleys and, as spring turned to summer and fall, foods in the higher mountains would also become ready to harvest. Deer and elk were taken and dried for winter use. Trout were caught in the creeks and mountain lakes.

Because there were no large man-made dams on the rivers, the Shasta made rock dams on the main channel of the rivers to help nature provide deeper pools of cool water for small fish and other river wildlife. In the fall, the salmon and steelhead left the safety of the Pacific Ocean and migrated upriver. At 2 to 4 feet long, they were much larger than the 8- to 16-inch trout. These larger migratory fish were caught in fish weirs. The dams that helped the small fish survive the hot summer now served another purpose. A trap woven of stick was leaned up against the rock dam. When the fish jumped the dam, they would hit the upright sticks and fall down into the pockets of the weir. The Shasta were able to take the fish they wanted and turn the rest loose to spawn or return to the ocean unharmed.

The Karuk, also spelled Karok or Kutuk, lived on the western side of Siskiyou County and further west into Del Norte County. The Karuk (upriver) occupied the mountains and middle section of the Klamath River drainage between the Yurok (downriver) to the west and the Upper Klamath-Shasta to the east. The Karuk were isolated much of the year from their neighboring tribes. The Klamath River canyon was their world and they survived on the bounty the land provided. They hunted large and small game, and gathered roots, berries, and healing herbs. They made baskets, weapons, clothing, medicines, canoes, bows, arrows, spears, and dip nets. They traded with the coast tribes for dentilia shells that they used for decorations and money, and with the Shasta for obsidian to be used for arrowheads, spear points, and knives.

The Karuk tribe was loosely held together, as much by their physical isolation from their neighboring tribes as by their relationships with each other. Shorter and darker than the Shasta, the Karuk lived along the Klamath River where very little flat ground interrupted the steep timber-covered slopes and jagged mountains that overlook the river canyon. The Klamath canyon provided mild winters along its narrow shores with snow rarely reaching the lower areas. In the cold winter months, steelhead and salmon were plentiful.

The Karuk called the Salmon River Quoratem and it is there, where the Salmon River meets the Klamath, that Kut-ah-min, or the center of the Karuk world, rises like Atlantis from the Klamath River canyon. Because the Klamath River splits, over the centuries it has cut channels between Kut-ah-min and the steep canyon walls to encircle the conical-shaped mountain. Their annual world renewal ceremony was revived in 1977.

The Karuk used "signal" trees near each village. High on a hill where they could be seen for miles, the two trees were always trimmed in the same pattern. One would be trimmed in the shape of a cross, and the other so only a small clump of growth was left at the top. Fires were built under these trees to communicate important messages, such as impending danger. The Karuk territory and language extended from Bluff Creek (called Ocketoh by the Karuk) to Clear Creek (Eenah-met). Clear Creek lies some 30 to 40 miles further up the river from the mouth of the Salmon River. Their territory also extended only a short ways up the Salmon River near the Wooley Creek drainage. The location is several miles down the Salmon River from the conflux of the north and south forks.

It is the Karuk words for the various tribes that we know today; they used the word *Youruk* (*Yurok*) for downriver Indians and *Kahruk* (*Karuk*) for themselves, meaning upriver Indians. The Yurok, on the other hand, called themselves the Peh-tsik (also meaning downriver). Their territory extended from the coast to Bluff Creek along the Klamath River. They called their Karuk neighbors up the Klamath River Poh-lik, which means upriver.

The Karuk were experts at dip netting salmon and steelhead along the series of waterfalls called Ishi Pishi Falls. Their houses were made of bark and other solid material. Often built over small pits, they were of lean-to design. The Karuk prided themselves on the quality and variety of designs and materials incorporated into their baskets and clothing. Animal hides, nuts, berries, seeds, quills, and various plant dyes were all used to create items that were used daily and could last indefinitely.

After the first trappers arrived in the Shasta Valley to the east, it took several years and arduous trips down steep canyons, over towering mountains and many wrong trails, before the trappers found Beaver Valley. There they found that the legends and stories told by the natives were true. Fur trappers were the first white people to make their fortunes in the small swampy valley surrounded by high mountains. The only way in or out was over the mountains or down a river. In only a few years' time, their trapping paradise would be invaded by an even larger, more aggressive group of people.

Stephen Hall Meek was the most famous trapper to enter Beaver Valley. Harvey E. Tobie recorded the following in his biography of Meek:

> Stephen Meek is more aptly describable as a Mountain Man than is his more famous younger brother Joseph. Although the latter devoted eleven years to mountain operations, he should be remembered essentially as a politician. Steve, on the other hand, never achieved lasting prominence in any public or private career. Though his activity was tremendous, his struggles brought him full circle into the mountains again; and there he died.

It was in 1830 that Stephen Meek enlisted with William Sublette. For years, he trapped and traveled the West, making him one of the original explorers of regions relatively unknown. In 1835, he joined Tom McKay, stepson of Dr. John McLoughlin of Hudson Bay Company. Early in the spring of 1836, Meek, McKay, and company "trapped their way beyond Fort Umpqua, along Klamath River, Scott River into Beaver Valley, and the Sacramento, returning by way of the American, Yuba, Pit, McLeod and Shasta rivers."

Meek traveled to the Black Hills, to Pike's Peak, and Taos, New Mexico, then back to Denver and Independence, where he visited his brother Hiram and sister Lusannah. According to Tobie, Meek's storytelling was so impressive that one woman, in hearing of his daring escapades, declared, "Law sakes! Mr. Meek, didn't you never get killed by none of them Indians and Bears?" To which Meek replied, "Oh, yes, madam, I was frequently killed."

A well-known trapper, scout, and guide, Meek led emigrant trains across the plains and, on May 11, 1845, met Elizabeth Schoonover, a 17-year-old Canadian-born woman. They were married on May 18, one week later. Though their fortunes rose and fell over the next years, the couple raised several children. Sadly, Elizabeth died from consumption in 1865 at age 37. Meek returned to his nomadic existence, carving out trails, trapping, guiding hunting parties, and acting as a consultant for historians of the period. Meek returned to Scott Valley and the Egli Ranch to live out the remainder of his life, hunting and trapping. Many knew him as an interesting, kind-hearted man. He died on January 11, 1889, and was buried in the Etna cemetery.

Soon after the gold rush began in 1849, it became apparent that California needed law and order. A government that was partly civilian and partly military was established. But that was not enough. Late in 1849, a convention was held and a state constitution was written. According to historians Lewis Paul Todd and Merle Curti, "The constitution outlawed slavery in California but included restrictions and discriminations against Indians. In 1850 Congress approved the constitution and California entered the union a free state."

Though California's Native Americans suffered under Mexican and Spanish rule earlier in the century, they suffered more terribly under American domination. The native population of the state rapidly declined; from 1848 to 1871, more than 50,000 Native Americans in California died due to violence,

STEPHEN MEEK. An early fur trapper of the Hudson Bay Company, Meek first visited Scott Valley in 1836. (Courtesy Fort Jones Museum.)

disease, starvation, and later, displacement. The Shasta, Karuk, Yurok, and Hupa tribes tried to fight back against the invading hordes, but when they succeeded in even minor victories, the outcry from the citizenry to deal with the Native Americans reached a fever pitch.

As a result, California had to make peace with the native populations. In April 1851, treaty makers were sent throughout the new state to appease the natives, who were being displaced, the gold-hungry miners, and the land-hungry settlers. The treaties were to be made on behalf of the United States government, but California was given only a small allowance. Incredibly, the treaty makers were given one year to complete the daunting task of traveling by foot and mule across California to make treaties with all known tribes. Colonel Reddick McKee was the leader of the expedition that traveled the northern part of California. Major Wessells, Colonel McKee's son John McKee, Secretary of the Commission Mr. Kelsey, Walter McDonald, Colonel Sarshel Woods, and a detachment of 35 riflemen were among the members of the group.

George Gibbs kept a journal of the expedition's travels through Indian country. In addition to his official documentation as record keeper for the company, he also noted people, points of interest, and personal observations. Commenting on the writing of Native American policy, Gibbs noted the following on page 144 of his journal:

KUTAMIN ON THE KLAMATH RIVER. The Karuk tribe's "center of the universe" was located at a site where the Salmon River meets the Klamath. (Courtesy Siskiyou County Museum.)

THE FIRST PEOPLE AND EARLY CONTACT

The policy early adopted by the Hudson's Bay Company—who, better than any other body of individuals, succeeded in the management of the Indians with whom they came into contact—was to break down the power and influence of petty chiefs, by placing in the hands of one man, of energetic character, and secured to their interests, the supreme control of the whole tribe; governing entirely through him, raising him to the rank of a white man, and giving him the means of supporting the dignity and state of which the savage is so fond. Such was their course with the COM-COMLEY, and with CASE-NAU; and such should be adopted in the treatment of the wild and turbulent nations of the Klamath and Trinity.

Before winter set in, Colonel McKee was to make treaties up the Russian River to its source, down the Eel River to Humboldt Bay, and over the mountains to the Klamath River where the expedition would proceed to Scott Valley. Starting on August 11, 1851, the treaty signers moved from one tribe to the next, picking up interpreters and guides to assist their safe passage. They reached the Trinity River in late September, averaging 10 to 12 miles of travel per day.

All tribes in the gold country had seen their population destroyed. Villages had been burnt along the trail and McKee suspected that, as they traveled further up the Klamath, they would see more devastation.

The treaty signed at Durkee's Ferry was made on October 6, 1851 with 12 bands of the Hoopa-Trinity and Klamath Indians. According to Gibbs, the tribes were granted a reservation that took 13 years to establish, but gave only the Hoopa tribe possession of the valley they still occupy today. Because the Karuk tribes could not be present, it was decided that their treaty would be signed as a supplement to Durkee's Ferry, further up the Klamath River canyon.

The men continued along the western side of the river, then over the mountain behind Big Bar. Four animals fell over the edge of the narrow trail; one horse survived the fall, but two mules broke their backs and a dragoon-horse was so injured, it was abandoned. When they reached Orleans Bar, it was nearly empty. It wasn't clear whether the miners had left due to clashes with the Native Americans or because they'd gone in search of richer diggings. The exhausted expedition, however, was grateful when they found that someone had planted a small garden and tomatoes were ripening on the vines.

On Saturday, October 11, the group arrived at a point about a mile above the mouth of the Salmon River and set up camp. The next day, a treaty was signed with bands of the Karuk near Kutamin, the center of their world, where the Salmon and Klamath Rivers meet. As noted by McKee, dated October 12, 1851 at Camp Quoratem, near the mouth of Salmon River, "I also leave with you (C.W. Durkee, Esquire, at Durkee's Ferry), for the Indians, a copy of the treaty made at your place on the 6th, with the supplementary treaty added here this day, in the arrangements made with the tribes near this camp." Now that these treaties were settled, the expedition headed up the Klamath River on October 13.

The next and final treaty for McKee's expedition would be in Scott Valley, some 100 miles further up the canyon trail where a dragoon of soldiers was attempting to keep order between the Shasta, the miners, and the early settlers. The expedition was to meet with representatives of the Upper Klamath, Shasta, and Scott Valley bands of the Shasta tribe. The trails improved due to the constant traffic created by pack trains transporting supplies to the mines along the Klamath, but with winter closing in, the expedition was eager to finish this leg of their journey. At Big Bar, the miners had already made a considerable find of gold. The whole bar had been excavated down to bedrock where deposits of nuggets had been found. There were no miners in sight, since they had abandoned the exhausted site for richer diggings.

The group reached the Scott River on October 21 and proceeded for 4 miles to Scott Bar. Gibbs noted that droves of diligent miners had mined the riverbanks, and "almost the whole river had been turned from its bed, and carried through canals, regularly built, with solid stone or log embankments, several feet in height and thickness." His account spoke of large gold pieces being found. One piece weighed 12 pounds and another was said to weigh 15 pounds troy. Small "coyote diggings," also known as "pocket mines," were thick along the riverbanks, but only 50 or so miners remained.

From a mountain ridge, the expedition spotted Scott Valley and Mount Shasta. After a 15-mile day, they reached the valley floor on October 22. Scott Valley stretches about 35 miles by 10 miles at its widest point. The land, at that time, was a swamp and seemed questionable for farming. The treaty makers soon learned that the arable land had already been claimed by squatters. To accommodate the squatters' rights and avoid including prime land or mining claims, McKee struggled to adjust the boundaries of the proposed reservation.

Kelsey was sent to Shasta Valley to invite the leaders of that band of Shasta to the treaty talks. He found little enthusiasm or cooperation in the wary people, who mistook his escort for a war party. Assumptions made by the expedition led to more misunderstanding and conflict.

Traditionally, the Shasta had a class system with elite and slave sects. The head chief reigned supreme and his many sons were sub-chiefs, who had presided over areas and bands of the tribe. The head chief, who been residing in Shasta Valley, was said to have recently died. McKee assumed that the disruption in tribal leadership would make his job considerably easier. With such dissent among the sub-chiefs, who were vying for supremacy, there was no guiding voice to make sure that the needs of all the people would be met. For 30 years, the Shasta had only to contend with a handful of fur trappers who caused few problems. Now, the Shasta lands were overrun with thousands of gold miners who churned up the rivers all year long, creating more turmoil than even the harshest winter storms. The deer and elk were taken by the hundreds to feed the miners, the vast majority of whom considered Native Americans an unpleasant distraction rather than fellow humans.

This knowledge, coupled with the confusion stirred by feuds over the selection of a head chief, led to a disruption in the relations between the Shasta of Scott

HAMBURG JOHN. He was one of the many Shasta who fled the region and ended up at Hoopa c. 1890. (Courtesy Siskiyou County Museum.)

Valley, Shasta Valley, the Klamath River, and the Rogue River in Oregon. Now, each sub-chief wanted peace, and the sooner the treaty could be signed and a reservation established, the sooner the people would be safe and well fed. This accomplished, the leaders could continue their internal battle to be the next head chief.

In a letter dated November 15, 1851, to C.C. Mix, acting commissioner of Indian affairs, Washington City, McKee notes that on "October 29th ultimo several additional parties of Indians reached my camp, and believing that by patiently waiting five or six days, an important treaty might be effected with the whole nation, precious as time was, I determined to remain, and at once took measures in relation to the vital question of a 'reservation.' "

Major Theodore F. Rowe, Charles McDermitt, Mr. Roach, and Dr. McKinney were some of the valley's early residents concerned with the proceedings and their own land claims. They came to McKee's camp to "give information and advice" and help negotiate equitable arrangements with the Shasta. McKee saw the wisdom in having miners and settlers involved in the treaty process. Because he could do nothing until the leaders of all bands of the Shasta could be convinced

19

AT THE SUMMIT. Travelers stop to take a breather near the top of Salmon Mountain, c. 1870. (Courtesy Siskiyou County Museum.)

that the negotiations weren't a trap, he dispatched messengers to Shasta Butte City (later renamed Yreka), and Scott Bar, and asked that representatives from their communities attend the treaty negotiations. This seems to be one of the few treaties where the local citizenry were actively involved on such a large scale. Their desires and needs were respected as much, if not more than, the Native Americans who were facing total extinction if an equitable treaty could not be made.

Because of their extensive land-base and reluctance to come forward, it was hard to calculate the actual number of Native Americans, but Gibbs estimated that the population to be included on the reservation would total "between four and six thousand souls."

The local citizenry immediately demanded compensation for loss of livestock and other material goods thought to have been stolen by Native Americans. They also demanded that their selected plots of land be excluded from the proposed reservation. Finally, they wanted every assurance that the hostile Native Americans would somehow be kept far from their doorsteps. With all this to contend with, McKee was beginning to regret his decision to include the white citizens in the delicate art of treaty making. Instead of expediting the process, he now could see no end to this treaty. Winter clouds began to gather on the horizon.

Because of the continued plundering and stealing, the whites further expressed that, as soon as winter set in, they were ready to "wage a war of extermination against the Indians on the Upper Klamath and its tributaries." For McKee, a treaty that would survive even a few months before bloodshed resumed seemed a far-off reality.

Fearing that impending winter storms would delay their travel, Major Wessels and the 35 riflemen left for Benicia on October 24, through the Sacramento canyon. He seemed confident that Colonel McKee had the situation well in hand, even though the whites were less than pleased with the possibility of a reservation displacing their claims to the land.

Shasta chiefs began to arrive with their entourages and the encampment on the east side of the valley grew to more than 1,000 Native Americans. McKee, Gibbs, and others scouted the valley and surrounding mountains to establish boundaries for the proposed reservation. Gibbs noted that "Sheep-rock," which lay between Shasta and Scott Valley, was one of the three places where big horn sheep were still known to live west of the Sierra Nevada range. It is now called Duzel Rock.

With their notes in hand, McKee, Gibbs, and Kelsey worked on securing a tract of land for the reservation. Since the chiefs were unable to say how many souls were under each one's authority, it was decided that the reservation would need to provide enough sustenance for those 4,000 or more Shasta who spoke the same language and lived along the Klamath, Shasta, Scott, Trinity, and Salmon Rivers. They also decided that a part of the Klamath River should be included, so the boundary was extended past the Klamath canyon and north to the Oregon border.

The miners and settlers were not pleased with the extent of the proposed reservation, and McKee deemed it impossible to create a reservation without displacing some whites. The settlers immediately submitted petitions to the agents, listing the hardships, loss of finances, and affected lands, all to be presented to the Indian Department of Congress. Promises of monetary compensation appeased most.

The Native Americans had wanted the entire Scott Valley, but when presented with the boundaries of the proposed reservation, readily agreed to move to the identified lands immediately. They further agreed to return all animals they had ever stolen from the whites. The Shasta were pleased that they would be instructed on how to deal with the whites in a fashion that would avoid further trouble. Many believed that once the gold ran out, the settlers would quickly leave, increasing the distance between the white and Native American population.

On the evening of November 3, there was a great celebration. The agents were treated to dances performed by the natives. On the afternoon of November 4, a peace treaty was signed by 13 Shasta chiefs and McKee. McKee later wrote that "a large bullock was killed for their supper."

Chief Ishack and his son were to escort McKee, Gibbs, McDonald, and three others back as far as Ishack's village on the Klamath River. On November 15, 1851, McKee wrote a letter to C.C. Mix from Durkee's Ferry, Klamath River:

> Through the blessing of Heaven, I trust that compact has accomplished
> what many intelligent persons thought an impossibility, and if prudently
> and successfully carried out, will save many valuable lives and perhaps

NED WICKS. Ned married Jenny Mungo, a Shasta chief's daughter, then left for Oregon but returned later in life. (Courtesy Betty Hall Collection.)

immense expense to the government. Unless I am greatly mistaken, the treaty of Scott's valley will be remembered, by both white and red men, long after the immediate parties to the arrangements have left the stage. . . . Thus ended a treaty arrangement with a large body of Indians who have ever been the dread, and not unfrequently the annoyance, of our people, since the first discovery of the northern mines, and with whom it may be predicted no amicable arrangements could be made. . . .

The Klamath river is undoubtedly rich in its deposits of gold; and before I left Scott's valley, several parties had already started for the purpose of prospecting its canons and bars, from which heretofore the Indian difficulties had shut them out. This is the best evidence of the confidence our people feel in the policy and permanence of the treaty. Upon the whole, I flatter myself that this arrangement, with those previously effected during this expedition, will restore and maintain quiet and security along this northern frontier.

John McKee agreed to stay in the valley to make sure that stolen property was returned to the whites and to supervise the Native Americans until Congress could adopt and officially create the reservation.

There is a large, unanswered question about the treaty signing and subsequent disappearance of many of the Shasta tribe: what happened to those who were to occupy this new reservation? While no known documents exist to validate the oral history related below, it is well known that some were sent to Siletz, Grand Rounde, and Klamath Reservations in Oregon. Others, seeing their way of life and freedom jeopardized, joined the army and became scouts. Whatever the case, in the Indian Census of 1852, it was reported that only 27 Shasta Indians were living in Siskiyou County.

The following has been passed down through several of the Shasta families. According to Fred Wicks, now deceased, a feast was prepared after the treaty was signed and the Shasta Indians were invited to eat. It was considered impolite and a sign of distrust, in the Shasta tradition, not to partake. As a result, most of the Shasta ate the beef and bread served. Whether from spoilage or poison, it isn't clear, but shortly after eating, the Shasta warriors began to die. It has been repeated in Shasta oral history that "3,000 warriors died that day." After that event, it was said by many that vigilantes, both miners and settlers, swept through the valleys burning the villages and killing the people.

Tyee ("chief" in Shasta) Jim was a young man in 1851 and, while he was allowed to observe the proceedings, he did not partake of the meal. He spoke until

JENNY MUNGO WICKS. Jenny married Ned Wicks and was the daughter of Chief Mungo, who signed a treaty in Fort Jones. (Courtesy Betty Hall Collection.)

his death, in 1908 at the age of 70, of "burying the dead along the trails." Because of his youth, Tyee Jim was not considered a threat and was allowed to return home to his village on Scott River.

Clara Wicks, born in the 1870s, in an interview with Terry Naylor, shared that her grandmother Jenny (Mungo) Wicks told her that "six-hundred didn't come home," meaning that 600 people she knew of never returned to Hamburg.

Chief Hiwashu, of a village just south of Yreka, was one who did make it home despite feeling ill. He had with him a copy of the treaty, written on buckskin. He told his family, "Bury this treaty with me for I want to take it to our god and know what kind of people we have made a treaty with."

Chief Sunrise, a treaty signer, had not eaten at the treaty signing. He fled to the mountains and hid from the whites for several years before he felt safe enough to return to Scott Valley and what remained of his tribe.

Chief "Ike" (Idakarawalkaha) was another treaty signer from the Klamath River near Jenny Creek. He also had refused to eat and survived to a very old age.

Fred Wicks, grandson of Jenny Mungo, spoke of working as a youth for Mr. Sharp, who owned Sharp's Gulch in Scott Valley. Sharp told young Fred of the roundup of the Shasta Indians a few short months after the treaty was signed. They were held in the livestock stockade at Fort Jones until they could be transported to Siletz and other reservations in Oregon. And the miners, 30 or so, came with their guns drawn to take back their women.

This scrap of history is borne out in the fact that the current tribe descends from fewer than 40 documented women who were kept by white miners, plus a half-dozen or so Native American couples. Some historians have attempted to dismiss the accumulated oral history of the Shasta, but the sad truth is that something did happen to the majority of the Shasta people. The mystery may never be solved since no written documentation exists to dispute it one way or the other. Ironically, after all the McKee expedition had endured to execute the treaties and identify the various tribes of northern California, McKee's efforts have still not been realized.

It wasn't long after the "signing" before the citizenry of Siskiyou County and other areas around California raised a cry to the state legislature about the injustice to law-abiding citizens and possible financial losses should the various treaties be ratified. Congress had allotted only limited funds and those had run out when McKee was making the treaty at Durkee's Ferry. The California legislature bowed to pressure and recommended to the United States Congress not to sign any of the treaties made after Durkee's Ferry. Eighteen of California's treaties were not ratified. They were put in an archive and sealed for 50 years.

Some 60 to 80 small allotments were given to Native Americans who lived a great distance from the white populations in Siskiyou. Many were old village sites where family groups had lived for centuries. Some parcels had old tribal burial grounds and were not of value to the miners or the farmers due to poor soil and/or water conditions. The unfortunate twist was that the Native Americans then couldn't provide crops for themselves and their way of life quickly changed from hunter/gatherers to laborers, working for the miners, or as farmhands, cooks, fur trappers, or at any other menial jobs that were offered.

In the meantime, Chief Shastika, who lived near Mount Shasta, was taken to a prison at Fort Miller. His wife, Blaze, and his daughters, Kate and Julia, fled to Salmon River to escape the vigilantes. Kate later married a miner, Josiah P. Jordan. She had a large family and her descendants still live in the Salmon River area today. Chief Kimolly, from Hamburg, spent 20 years on Alcatraz, coming home in his later years.

In 1874, there was another attempt to create a reservation for the Shasta. The plan was to set aside land in Quartz Valley and north, up to the Oregon Border. When told of this plan, Shasta families hoped that the reservation, with ample farmland and water, would materialize. A small group on Wildcat Creek abandoned their small government allotment that was then bought up by their white neighbors. Unfortunately, the proposed reservation plan was also derailed and the Native Americans who had given up their allotments had to find homes in the white community.

If history could be rewritten, hopefully it would be by those who believe in the ideals of Americanism. Sadly, the irony lives on in McKee's haunting words: "Results will, I hope, promote the interest of the Indian tribes . . . [and] the peace and prosperity of the State, and . . . carry out the benevolent policy of our government."

NELLIE REUBEN. An Indian woman from Salmon River, Nellie was great-grandmother to Helen Lincoln of Etna, California, who was the daughter of the oldest mail courier in the United States. (Courtesy Siskiyou County Museum.)

2. THE FIRST GOLD SEEKERS

The first gold seekers to Western Siskiyou County followed the waterways, in particular the Klamath River and its tributaries. A land of rugged mountain ranges and steep gorges, the only semblance of an earlier trail led to Oregon, a remnant of the Hudson Bay trapping era. That trail meandered up the Sacramento River, through Shasta Valley, across the Klamath River, and over the Siskiyou Mountains into Oregon.

This was not the route the original Siskiyou argonauts traveled. Most of these men, primarily young men under the age of 30 who had become frustrated by the waning deposits in the Sierras, sought new diggings. Traveling up the California coast or down from Oregon, they discovered the Trinity River where prospects looked good. One miner, Major Reading, having left Coloma in the Mother Lode with nothing to show for it, took out $80,000 along the Trinity.

Prospectors also traveled up from the mouth of the Klamath River. In H.H. Bancroft's *History of Oregon*, the first likely discovery of gold cited on the Klamath River occurred in the spring of 1850 at Salmon Creek and, in July 1850, on the main Klamath. In September, gold was discovered on Scott River. General Joseph Lane, arriving from Oregon, discovered gold on the Shasta River in 1850, near where the town of Yreka now stands.

The second group of miners to permeate the region was led by John W. Scott, whose name was then given to a valley, a river, and a mountain pass. He and his men discovered gold at Scott Bar in July or August 1850. And later, as reported in the *Sacramento Union* for June 23, 1851: "The largest lump of pure gold ever found in California was taken out by Messrs. Brown, Beach and Forest at Scott Bar on Scott River within the last few weeks and weighed $3,140.00." It was reportedly free of "spot or blemish."

Scott Bar yielded richly, as revealed by an article appearing in the March 18, 1854 *Mountain Herald*: "The bed of the stream has proved exceedingly rich, and has been worked with immense profit every summer since its discovery. It is not, nor will it be exhausted for many years. It is a stream of 'heavy strikes.' " In a short time, Scott Bar became a lively mining town with more than 50 residences, as well as stores, boarding houses, saloons, a butcher shop, a blacksmith, a hotel, even a drugstore. The cemetery dates back to 1857. Some of the early miners and settlers

MAP OF THE NORTHERN MINES. In its heyday, this region of countless gold mines saw the removal of more than $20 million.

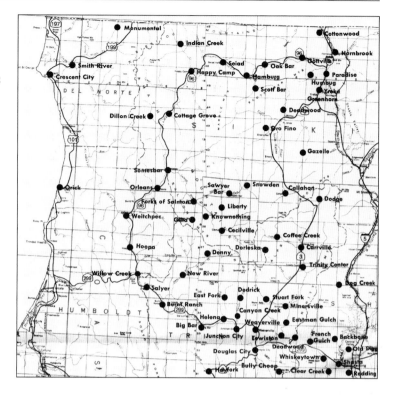

included Joseph Barney Leduc and Richard "Dick" Hetchel. Others included the Milne, Nesbitt, Simon, Noonan, and Andrews families.

While J.W. Scott and his men continued along Scott River, another group of miners prospected the Klamath River from its mouth up to the Shasta River in the spring of 1850. The following is reported according to David Rys Jones:

> It was this group of miners that established the course of the Klamath River below the junction of the Shasta. From that time on, the river that had been variously known as the Clamette, the Klamet, Indian Scalp River, and Smith River, has borne the name by which it was known near its source.

Prospectors from Trinity River likewise mined the Salmon River region as early as June of 1850. They established a small post or settlement there—the first—called Bestville in honor of Captain Best, a sea captain, miner, and trader who discovered gold with the help of Squirrel Jim, a Shasta Indian who became a "friend" to many whites. (When Squirrel Jim died in 1919, he was buried on the Sallie Burcell allotment in Etna. He died from "the infirmities of old age" and was "about 100 years old.")

The richest and most extensive discovery north of the Trinity range of mountains was found near Yreka, but this site was ignored for several months

ARRASTRA. Used to separate gold, this was a more sophisticated method of extraction. (Courtesy Trinity County Historical Society.)

until a party from Oregon camped at Yreka Flats, a popular camping ground between the Shasta and Scott Rivers. Most miners passing through were so intent on getting to the streambeds, they never dreamed that gold lay just below the surface of the ground—literally beneath their feet. But one day in March 1851, Abraham Thompson did do a little scratching; "After washing three pans of dirt beside a small ravine, later called Black Gulch, a good prospect of coarse gold was found . . . He took it to his companions and finding 'little scales of gold clinging to the roots of the long grass,' convinced them 'of the richness of their find.' " It didn't take long for Thompson's Dry Diggings to mushroom into a tent city, first known as Shasta Butte City, then renamed Yreka. Within six months, there were 5,009 men vying for 30-foot claims, as well as the water that became more valuable than gold.

J.A. Cardwell, an early miner in Yreka, wrote the following in 1879:

> . . . prospecting was carried on vigorously all that year [1851]. Humbug Creek some eight miles from Yreka was struck in the spring and it all was immensely rich and afford room for a great many men to work. I was acquainted with a man by the name of Jones that took out $95,000 on Humbug that summer.

Humbug Creek, a tributary to the Klamath, was the site of one of the first quartz veins found in Siskiyou County. In 1852, a few arrastras and a mill were built. The poet-miner Joaquin Miller, who lived at Humbug during the 1850s, described a day in the life of a miner:

> Now the smoke from the low chimneys of the log cabins began to rise and curl through the cool, clear air on every hand, and the miners to come out at the low doors; great hairy, bearded, six foot giants, hatless, and half-dressed. They stretched themselves in the sweet, frosty air, shouted to each other in a sort of savage banter, washed their hands and faces in the gold-pan that stood by the door, and then entered their cabins again, to partake of the eternal beans and bacon and coffee, and coffee and bacon and beans.

A short distance away, the community of Yreka took root, beside Yreka Creek and not far from Greenhorn Creek, which empties into Yreka Creek. According to J. Roy Jones in *Saddle Bags in Siskiyou*, W.W. Powers built the first house in Yreka, on Miner Street.

T.J. Roach, a correspondent for the San Francisco *Alta California*, wrote the following on November 10, 1851:

> A few weeks ago I visited Shasta Butte City [Yreka]. I was much surprised to find such a large town on the very frontiers of California. I counted over two hundred and fifty frame houses up and occupied during a stroll through the streets, and ladies, dressed a la "Bloomer" perambulated the streets, showing a state of civilization quite unparalleled in these wild parts.

In 1852, Jacob Wagner wrote to his sister and brother back in Iowa:

> There are about four or five thousand persons in Shasta Butte City [Yreka] and within ten miles of here, some living in brush houses, others in tents . . . There are about 30 stores and about the same number of gambling houses and liquor shops. We are about 300 miles from navigation. The provisions we get here are packed 300 miles on mules . . . At present, flour is 25 cents a pound, beans 20 cents, coffee 50 cents, butter $1.25, boots from $8.00 to $16.00 a pair, potatoes 25 cents a pound, liquor 50 cents a drink.

By 1853, however, prices were soaring. The following correspondence came from a letter written by Captain Alden of Fort Jones to his wife on May 31, 1853,

> Everything comes . . . [to Scott Valley] by pack trains at 20 cents a pound from Shasta City [Redding] . . . Butter is $2 a pound, eggs $3 a dozen,

hams $5 a piece, potatoes $15 a bushel [by June 6th he was paying $22 a bushel; by June 9th, $24 a bushel]. And a cat costs here and at Yreka (16 miles northeast) six dollars, and a hen is $5.00.

Several log or plank homes were built in Yreka in the first year, along with a hotel built by Mr. and Mrs. David H. Lowry (or Lowery). Mrs. Lowry is credited with being "the first white woman to settle in the county." This couple next moved to Scott Valley, where they helped established the first church, the Crystal Creek Methodist Church, in 1854. David H. Lowry became the lay minister.

Joaquin Miller described Yreka's main street this way:

A tide of people poured up and down, and across from other streets, as strong as in a town of the East. The white people on the side walks, the Chinese and mules in the main street. Not a woman in sight, not a child, not a boy. Brick houses on either hand, two and three stories high. A city of altogether, perhaps, five thousand souls.

Another of the community's most famous residents during its early years was the young Miss Lotta Crabtree. Born in New York in 1847, she and her mother followed her father out to California around 1851. They settled in La Porte, but soon moved up to the northern mines, landing in Deadwood, "over the Greenhorn divide from Yreka." Mrs. Crabtree then moved to Yreka with Lotta. A quick and lively child, Lotta began performing at the Arcade Saloon. The miners idolized her, tossing her coins and little gold nuggets. After two years of living in Yreka and performing all over Siskiyou County, Lotta and her mother moved on. She joined a musical troupe, settling for a time in San Francisco. Eventually, Lotta toured the nation, but Yrekans still point out where the Arcade Saloon once stood and where "Topsy" performed.

Large numbers of miners rushed to Western Siskiyou County during the first half of the 1850s with little more than pick and shovel or pan. Within a few years, however, new technology was introduced. One such improved technique was the long tom. With it, men, banding together in companies of six or eight, could process four to five times more gravel. Another innovation was the sluice, which, though even simpler in design than a long tom, was more effective in extracting gold.

As the population swelled, pack trains began criss-crossing the rugged terrain of Western Siskiyou's mountain ranges, becoming the lifeline to the area. The May 14, 1851 *Sacramento Union* reported, "Over 1000 pack mules left here again today loaded for the northern mines."

Trails were steep and narrow, and had to be cut through forests of white fir and pine. Boulders had to be moved and bridges were little more than trees dropped across streams. The constant threat of Native American attack kept everyone nervous. Before long, the most important established route—shorter than the Sacramento River Trail—began at Fort Reading, meandered through mountains, over Scott Mountain, and into Scott Valley. From there, it continued north along Scott River up to Wheelock's trading post (later replaced by Fort Jones), then followed Cherry Creek or McAdams Creek north to Deadwood. From Deadwood, the trail crossed over to Thompson's Dry Diggings near Yreka. A second trail branched off of the main trail through Scott Valley near the Ohio House and, from there, the trail crossed Scott River, continuing west along the foothills to Aetna Mills and Rough and Ready. Finally, the trail crossed into the Salmon Mountains. The trail from Trinidad on the coast to the junction of the Salmon and Klamath Rivers was also six days of hard travel.

Mules—numbering 30 to 60 or more—went through as often as could be arranged. From 1849 to 1856, they constituted the sole form of transportation in and around Siskiyou County. Before long, 2,000 pack mules were traversing the narrow, rugged, and often snowy trails each year. According to H.L. Wells, the leading packers in the early days included Jerome Churchill, Silas Parker, James Knuff, S.C. Horsley, Frank Drake, Thompson and Wood, Batterton and Hickman, John William Burgess, Augustus Meamber, Jones, Orr, and Townsend. Others, such as Elijah Steele, and Sloan, Briggs, and Tiernan, began a freight express line that ran from Scott Bar to Yreka and Sacramento. Steele rode express. Gus Meamber packed in and out on the Old Kelsey Creek Trail to Happy Camp and the Klamath River.

LOTTA CRABTREE. The "Darling of the Goldfields," young Lotta lived in Yreka for two years and performed throughout the region before moving on. (Courtesy Siskiyou County Museum.)

SNOWDEN PACK TRAIN. These mules are packed and ready to travel over Salmon Mountain to Etna. (Courtesy Betty Young Collection.)

Roads were eventually forged and cleared, and tolls were collected. The Scott-Shasta Valley Turnpike, first established in the late 1850s, remained a toll road until 1864. "Yank" Johnson, the toll keeper, collected the $2 toll on top of Forest (House) Mountain (also known as Yreka Mountain). A toll was also collected at the Forest House, the stage stop on the eastern side of the mountain. In 1864, however, a group of citizens paid $3,000 to free up the road; owners of the Forest House contributed $1,600.

The Forest House, built in 1852, was not the only popular stage and rest stop on the new roads dissecting the region. The Forks of Salmon Hotel was built in 1851, and it boasted a butcher shop, bar, kitchen, dining room, and eight rooms upstairs with an additional room with ten beds. The American House (also called the Dodge House) and Callahan's Ranch Hotel also accommodated the increasing number of miners, packers, and settlers.

One important stopping point along the North Fork of the Salmon River, still known as Sawyer's Bar, was established a mile above Bestville in Trooks Flat. It served as a hub to other bustling settlements up and down the river and nearby creeks. Here Dan Davis, Sawyer's Bar's first blacksmith, sharpened picks on a big rock he used as an anvil, charging $1 per point. A. Trooks had a large store here in 1851.

Sawyer's Bar remained an important settlement for another 50 years or more. One of its most interesting landmarks is the Catholic church built on Paradise Flat. It is one of the few places within the Klamath National Forest to be listed on the National Register of Historic Places. The building dates to 1855, its construction supervised by a Benedictine Monk from Austria, Father Florian S. Schwenninger, who arrived in 1853. A devout man, he brought with him a painting of Christ's crucifixion that hung above the altar. In addition, Father Florian built the altar himself. Now almost 150 years old, it is the oldest Catholic church in northern California and the second oldest church built in Siskiyou County. It has often been said that the small structure sits on the richest piece of real estate, since it is the only section of land around Sawyer's Bar never to have been mined.

Other Salmon River mining sites included Forks of Salmon, Yocumville, Cecilville, Russianville, Black Bear, Petersburg, and Somes Bar. Forks of Salmon, located at the junction of the North and South Forks, was mined as early as 1850. An important supply center, there was also a sawmill (constructed by a Mr. Johnson), a two-story hotel (constructed by a Mr. Long), bars, and a store. A post office was built in 1858. Early families residing here included the Bennett and George families, whose descendants still work and live in the area.

Yocumville, established in 1856 opposite the mouth of Methodist Creek, also had a sawmill, built by J.B. Yocum and Joseph Ritner, and a flume that carried

SAWYER'S BAR CHURCH. First built in 1855, this was the earliest Catholic church in the northern region and is still in use today. (Courtesy Siskiyou County Museum.)

water to mines on the South Fork of the Salmon River. The first store and pack train was owned by Phil Dunphy. Here, the Fyfield family owned and operated an inn and store that serviced miners and travelers. According to Lida Fyfield, "Our inn was very large—two stories in front and three in back . . . We had a large vegetable garden, berries, and many fruit trees. We raised our own beef and in the fall about one hundred hogs were driven in from Scott Valley, butchered, and made into hams, bacons, sausage, etc. . . . All our [other] supplies for the store and house were brought in by pack trains." All that remains of Yocumville today are some old rock foundations.

Cecilville, supposedly named for John B. Sissel, became a trading center for miners along the South Fork of the Salmon River. Russianville, established by a colony of Russian miners, was located at the junction of the Little North Fork and the North Fork of the Salmon River. Black Bear, established in the 1860s, became an important trading center, with a 32-stamp mill, sawmill, school, post office, even housing for 300 men plus their families.

Petersburg, settled in the 1850s and 1860s, was, for a time, the largest settlement along the 16-mile stretch of the South Fork of Salmon River between Abrams at Big Flat and Cecilville. Built on a sunny gravel bar, it boasted a hotel, stores, saloons, a meat shop, blacksmith, sawmill, corrals, many residences, even orchards and gardens irrigated by water from nearby gulches and ditches. J.P. Jordan, with ranches at Rush Creek and Garden Gulch, supplied the town with fresh beef. Others who ran businesses or pack trains through here included Arnold Nordheimer, W.P. Bennett and his partner Peter Miller, Kist and Davis, George H. Sightman, George Green Brown, George Wohlfert, Francis Abrams, and Thomas McGinnis Brown, who worked as sheriff of Klamath County for 14 years. A substantial Chinese community grew up at the lower end of Petersburg, the only section of the community to survive after being mined away by the Salmon River Hydraulic Mining Company at the turn of the century.

Somes Bar, located two miles above the mouth of the Salmon River, was settled by Abraham Somes around 1860. It thrived for 40 years, but was eventually abandoned.

Lesser known sites along the Salmon River included Summerville, mined almost exclusively by Chinese miners in the latter part of the 1890s; Gilta, serving both placer and quartz mines along Knownothing Creek; Rollin, not developed until the 1890s; and Shadrick's, site of a Chinese camp, located at the mouth of Shadow Creek. In Scott Valley and Quartz Valley, there were important settlements as well.

At the southern end of Scott Valley lay Callahan's (also called Callahan's Ranch and then Callahan). Near the junction of the East and South Forks of Scott River, it became a rest stop for pack trains crossing Scott Mountain. At the same time, the South Fork contributed much of the placer gold found on the upper Scott River. Mathias B. Callahan is credited with establishing the site of the Callahan Ranch Hotel. In Ernest Hayden's *Along our History's Trail*, Mary Callahan wrote that her father brought the family over the Trinity Mountains en route to Yreka,

CALLAHAN HOTEL AND PARADE. Old Callahan Days celebrates the mining days of the past. The stone monument in front of the hotel was hauled out of the mountains by Tuffy and Harry Fowler in 1948. (Courtesy Homer Barandun Collection.)

but while crossing the East Fork of the Scott River, her pregnant mother was swept downstream. Soon rescued, she was taken to a cabin owned by a Frenchman, but went into early labor and gave birth to a son. The infant was so weak he was "kept warm in the Frenchman's brick bake oven."

While forced to stay with the Frenchman, Mathias saw what kind of business opportunity lay in this strategic location. The two men bartered and the Frenchman sold Mathias his cabin for two mules and some supplies. Callahan and his wife then built up the place so people could "stay all night and eat." When he sold out to Asa White, Masterson, and Lytle, they built the landmark Callahan's Ranch Hotel. Constructed of hand-hewn logs, it became a popular and famous stop.

After a few years, Callahan also sold his ranch, located nearby, to Lucius Stafford Wilson and finally moved his family to Yreka. In 1873, Richard Vose Hayden bought Wilson's ranch (in Noyes Valley) and Callahan's Ranch Hotel. The post office was in the hotel at that time and Hayden was the postmaster. The hotel is still standing today, though it has been boarded up for many years. The town of Callahan remained lively for another couple decades, with a population ranging from 500 to 1,500 people.

Other important Callahan landmarks include Farrington's Store, the Emporium (originally the Baker Hotel), the old Callahan Church (built in 1855), and the Grange Hall, which once housed the original Denny-Bar Company Store. Built in 1864 by Tom, Joe, and Albert Denny, it became the first of a series of local chain stores. In Siskiyou County alone, there were at least eight Denny-Bar Stores.

Stephen Farrington built the original Farrington structure back in the 1860s. Beginning with a blacksmith shop at the south end, he added a saloon and, finally, a hotel linking the structures together. Farrington's, though closed today, is still owned by the original Farrington family.

At the northern end of Scott Valley, O.C. Wheelock established one of the most important trading centers in the area. According to Harry L. Wells, a cabin that was first built in 1851, presumably by Brown and Kelley, was sold to Wheelock and company, including Captain John B. Pierce, a Mr. Fouts, and John and Stephen Watson. It was Wheelock, however, who took over the trading post and house of public entertainment. This station—also known at other times as Scottville, Scottsburg, or Ottitiewa (which was the name of the Scott Valley branch of the Shasta Indians), and later renamed Fort Jones in 1860—was located beside what would become the trail from Yreka to Shasta.

An interesting landmark, built in 1851 and still standing in Fort Jones, was the Fort Jones House. In 1976, it was listed in the National Register of Historic Places. An important stage stop and hotel on the California-Oregon stage route,

FORT JONES SKETCH. *This early sketch shows the original Fort Jones, which was established in 1852 and dismantled ten years later. (Courtesy Sara Whipple Collection.)*

it was also a "pleasure house" used by soldiers garrisoned at the new fort. Unique to this house, however, is its walls. Made to look like stonework, the "rusticated wood" or "wood siding [was] cut to look like stone and painted with a special paint containing sand." Along with the Fort Jones House, this type of unique siding can be seen at George Washington's Mount Vernon.

Not far from Wheelock's stood the new army fort, Fort Jones. Named for Colonel Roger Jones, adjutant general of the army from 1825 to 1852, Fort Jones was garrisoned by Company E 4th U.S. Infantry in October 1852, under the command of Captain (Brevet Major) Edward H. Fitzgerald. In the beginning there were only a couple of log buildings with dirt floors, but by 1854, there were a total of nine structures, described in the following manner:

> . . . seven are of unhewn logs and two of rough boards. Two of the log buildings, two rooms each, are occupied as officers quarters, one log building as Company quarters and mess room, a fourth log building as laundress's quarters and Guard House, a fifth as an Hospital and the other two log houses are kitchens to officer's quarters. The two frame buildings are Subsistence and Quartermaster Store House, Stable and Granary. The log houses, daubed with mud, good roof and floored, except the one in which the Guard Room is, which has no floor and a bad roof, are quite comfortable and with the present force at the Post are barely sufficient in size and number.

General George Crook, who later gained fame during the Civil War, was stationed at Fort Jones when he first left West Point. It is said that General Ulysses S. Grant and Phillip Sheridan were also assigned duty at Fort Jones, but never arrived. The fort was built to protect miners and settlers from Native American attack. "Old Man Ruffy," a Shasta who died in 1930 at more than 110 years of age, reported the following:

> A number of white men . . . built a long log house [Fort Jones] with many round holes on each side of the building. The white men put holes on each side of the building. The white men put guns through the holes and killed the Indians . . . Then one day, a Big Man came to the log house. He wore nice clothes and had ribbons on coat and each side of pants. Big Man took lots of men with him on horses and go all over the valley killing Indians. Lots of Indians ran away and never came back. After the Big Man left the Indians did not fight any more because they were afraid Big Man come back.

Ironically, Ruffy was buried with an old American flag draped over his coffin, a flag he had come to cherish over the years. He served as the first person to ever haul mail over Salmon Mountain. In addition, in order to preserve some of his tribe's songs, he agreed to record them on wax cylinders that William J. Balfrey provided. Though already over 100 years old, Ruffy was thrilled when he heard the Shasta stories preserved for the future.

Hostilities with the Shasta were brought under control within the first years of settlement. As indicated in the first chapter of this book, controversial and undocumented data exists concerning a possible poisoning of a large number of Shasta in the early years. Whatever is the truth is hard to determine as there is little to authenticate what might have happened. At any rate, by the mid-1850s, relations between the army and the Shasta were improving, at least in the eyes of the U.S. Army. Correspondence from the fort supports the fact that there were fewer encounters with local Shasta, even though other violent encounters continued to occur throughout the region for many years.

In a piece of correspondence dated August 12, 1855, Captain H.M. Judah, writing to Major E.D. Townsend at Benicia, wrote:

> The Scott's Valley Indians are brave, generally young and would make troublesome foes. At the same time they are easily controlled, if not interfered with by the whites, the course pursued by the late Agent and the Military having succeeded in securing their entire confidence in them; this confidence it is my endeavor to retain, and can do so if the settlers and miners could be made amenable to any law for their cruel, barbarous and inhuman treatment of them. In acts of atrocity they have in some instances surpassed the savage himself, and until these things can be checked or the Indians removed from all intercourse with them, so long must these disturbances ensure.

Trouble, however, with Native Americans outside the area continued to occur frequently. In 1856, ten miners were killed along the Klamath River by a band of visiting Indians. When news of the attack reached the garrison, a large posse tracked the native group back to the Rogue River in Oregon. A disagreement with Captain Andrew J. Smith, the Fort Lane (southern Oregon) commandant over jurisdiction, led the Californians to return to Yreka to obtain warrants. Some months later, the wanted men were caught and delivered to Siskiyou County. The accused were hanged.

By March 1856, the Oregon Rogue River War was "raging in earnest." Inevitably, Fort Jones was drawn into conflicts outside the county. Under Lieutenant George Crook, Company E, 4th Infantry was called into duty, reporting to Captain Smith at Fort Lane. At one point, Crook, who had been incapacitated by rheumatism and was bedridden, returned to the field to find that two-thirds of his company had been killed or wounded by Native Americans. The Rogue River War finally ended when the hostile band surrendered and was returned to the Yamhill Agency.

In early winter 1856, the Pitt River Indians, in the northeastern part of California and near the Nevada border, rose up against settlers in the Pitt River Valley. Captain Judah, with First Lieutenant George Crook, led both Company E and D of the Fort Jones garrison into the field. Reportedly, because Fort Jones was no longer a cavalry unit, there were not enough suitable mounts, thus the men saddled up what available pack mules they could and headed out. The following account details these improvisations:

> [Some mules had to be borrowed from nearby residents and] . . . accoutrements were improvised on the spot . . . some with ropes, and others with equally, if not worse, makeshifts to fasten the saddles on the mules . . . It was as good as a circus to see us when we left Fort Jones. Many of our men were drunk, including our commander [Judah]. Many of the mules were wild, and had not been accustomed to being ridden, while the soldiers were generally poor riders. The air was full of soldiers after the command was given to mount, and for the next two days stragglers were still overtaking the command.

COLONEL BREVETT JONES. This is the man for whom Fort Jones was named. (Courtesy Betty Hall–Irene Jordan Nelson Collection.)

DEADWOOD DEDICATION. In 1948, a rock monument was established at Deadwood, the mining site and town that lost the county seat by one or two votes. Nothing exists on the site today. (Courtesy Fort Jones Museum.)

Later, George Crook was wounded, receiving an arrow in his hip, but he refused to leave his command or return to Fort Jones, the site of the nearest doctor. Instead, he sent word back to Fort Jones for Doctor C.C. Kearney to come to him. In addition to sending the doctor, Captain Judah—who was too drunk to travel himself—sent reinforcements. Crook recovered from his wound and returned to action. A series of campaigns followed until July 1857, at which time Crook was ordered to leave Siskiyou County and travel up to Klamath Lake country, home of the Modoc and Rock Indians, where a new outpost was being established. In October 1857, George Crook headed out.

Fort Jones was dismantled in 1858, but not officially abandoned until General Order No. 21 in August of 1866. Native American trouble, though not over, had been reduced. That, along with the intensifying conflict between the North and South, made the army's presence in northern California less important. Today, nothing remains of the fort except a single frame house that was long ago moved into town and converted into a residence. However, three men stationed at the fort during its short term included Sergeant James Bryan, Sergeant John Griffin, and Private Gundor Salverson. After their discharges in the early 1850s, they settled in Scott Valley. Today, the descendants of Bryan still ranch on the eastern side of the valley.

Deadwood grew up around the junction of Deadwood and Cherry Creeks during the summer of 1851. These two creeks flow into McAdams Creek (named for a Scotsman who mined here) and finally the Scott River. Folklore has it that a prospector, making a new discovery, looked down and noted a dead tree near the creek, so he called the site Deadwood. By 1853, there was a store and butcher shop owned by William Davidson, plus a trading post owned by William Pool. In the spring of 1854, though smallpox took its toll, C.H. Pyle opened a second butcher shop in Pool's trading post. Two log houses and one shake house were also erected in the town proper. When rich diggings were found along McAdams Creek nearby, more and more miners swarmed to the area. Deadwood became a great center of activity, second only to Yreka in regional importance. In 1856, a county convention was held here, but Deadwood lost the bid for county seat by two votes. By 1857, there were three stores, two stables, three saloons, two hotels, a blacksmith, a butcher shop, a bakery, a dairy, and several residences.

Ironically, Deadwood's fame receded nearly as quickly as it rose as Fort Jones, a thriving new community in the valley below, competed for business and trade. In addition, on Thursday morning, December 26, 1861, a large fire burned down most of Deadwood's structures, and later fires destroyed the little that remained. Today, there is only a stone monument heralding the life of this raucous community and a minimum security honor camp 5 miles up McAdams Creek.

A short distance from McAdams Creek, along Indian Creek, another community was established. Perhaps as early as 1853 or 1854, W.G. Rider, having traveled from Deadwood, began prospecting along the creek. The only other miners reportedly in the area before this included a band of black miners, a small Boston company, and a miner named Joseph Barker who had taken up residence in Grizzly Gulch.

When Rider returned to Deadwood, he shared what he believed were good prospects. As a result, Horace Knights took a pack train over to Indian Creek and set up camp at Hi You Gulch. He constructed a temporary store and built a log house. By Christmas of that year, more than 300 miners had moved into the area. In 1855, another store was built downstream. This second location, more popular than the first, was called Hooperville in honor of Frank Hooper. A school was established, as well as a post office and a baseball team. Hooperville remained an active community for many years, its population swelling to 4,000 or more in 1854. By 1881, only a handful of Chinese miners remained.

Clearly, by 1851, gold was being discovered in every part of Western Siskiyou County and people from around the globe were flocking to the area. Estimates reveal that, in 1849, foreign gold seekers constituted nearly 25 percent of the non-Native American population in California; by 1860, that rose to 40 percent. In January 1850, there were approximately 800 Chinese immigrants in California; by 1851, there were at least 4,000. By the end of 1852, though Chinese made up only 10 percent of the state's population, the 20,000 to 25,000 immigrants constituted a highly visible minority. They did not arrive in Siskiyou County in reportable numbers, however, until the spring of 1853.

The Chinese miners worked diligently on claims others abandoned. They worked for lower wages than whites, too, usually $1.25 to $1.50 a day, which added to the contempt many whites felt. Most of the Chinese miners came with little more than a pan or rudimentary tools, but they aptly learned to make do, creating rockers from split sections of oak trees or sieves from perforated deerskins. They also formed small corporations, which appeared to many to undermine the individual white miner's independence and opportunity, as expressed by this *Shasta Courier* editorial: "What must be his (the American miner) feelings to find himself suddenly surrounded and hemmed in on every side by a motley swarm of semi-barbarians, eager to grasp the spoils." Fear of this strange newcomer continued to grow.

Clearly, whites believed that the wealth of California's mines should be reserved for white Americans and northern Europeans. A miner's tax first instituted in 1850 was revised in 1852. The tax amounted to $3 a month in 1852 to be increased to $4 a month in 1853, coupled with property seizure for those who didn't comply. In 1854, there was a move to increase the tax, but much to the amazement of many, the state Foreign Miner's Tax was repealed instead. Regardless of the repeal, illegal seizures routinely took place, and whites posing as tax collectors robbed Chinese miners.

Throughout California, antagonistic and discriminatory policies were initiated. Chinese miners were voted out of Columbia's gold fields in 1852, while a California court proclaimed that no Chinese could testify against a white man in court, unless substantiated by a white witness. In Siskiyou County, restrictive policies toward the Chinese were also passed and enforced. One of the first efforts to exclude Chinese from immigrating into California actually took place in Yreka as early as 1855, but the first real violence against the Chinese did not break out until July 4, 1856, during Yreka's Fourth of July celebration.

Patriotic celebration turned into drunken revelry when a group of miners marched down to Yreka's "Chinatown" and began kicking in doors, beating up men, and assaulting women. Both Chinese (there were very few) and white women were attacked, as local prostitutes lived in the same part of town. Eventually, Deputy Sheriff Millhouse arrived and advised the rioters to stop. John Blunt, one rowdy miner, refused. When the deputy tried to arrest him, Millhouse and Blunt began fighting. Millhouse was brutally beaten by Blunt, taking blows to the head and face, nearly blinding him. When Millhouse drew his gun and fired three times, a bullet struck Blunt and killed him. The miners immediately called for a hanging, but the deputy escaped to the safety of the jailhouse.

It didn't take long for miners from all over the county to rush to Blunt's defense and a trial was held; though Millhouse was acquitted on grounds of self-defense, his friends knew he'd never be safe. They collected $600 and the deputy fled Yreka to Pennsylvania. He never returned. In the meantime, the *Yreka Union* published a special edition headline, supporting Millhouse and decrying the actions of the miners. The miners threatened to tar and feather the editor, but nothing ever occurred. Relations with the Chinese, however, did not improve.

CHINESE MINER, DEADWOOD. This Chinese miner named Song was photographed working in his garden c. 1890. (Courtesy Fort Jones Museum.)

Etna's early history began in response to the growing need to feed and supply miners. Because staples had to be hauled in by mule train and because the heavy winter snows made travel difficult and dangerous, in 1853, several enterprising men gathered together and built a sawmill on what would later become Etna's Main Street. They had to dig a ditch from Etna Creek to the mill to furnish water. One of the owners built the first house not far away. Early the next year, a flour mill was also built on Etna Creek, near the foot of Salmon Mountain. Captain Charles McDermitt, Charles Moore, William and Dr. Davidson bought grain produced on the nearby Davidson Brothers' Farm, then later bought grain from other valley farmers. Mrs. David H. Lowry (or Lowery), wife of the minister of Crystal Creek Church, reportedly named the mill Aetna Mills. A second flour mill, a mile away, was built in 1855 by a group of farmers, including Abisha Swain, H.C. Swain, Obediah Baer, George Smith, P.A. Hartstrand, and James Stevens. James Stevens named this mill the Rough and Ready Mill. Abisha Swain and E.R. Herby were the first to build their homes nearby.

Around each of these mills grew two small towns, one called Aetna Mills, the other Rough and Ready. Other buildings were raised, including a hotel in Aetna Mills built by the Davidson brothers, later operated by Fitzsimmons and Neilon. A sawmill, a blacksmith shop, a machine shop, two stores, a couple of saloons, a furniture store, and a post office were also established there. A distillery was built

MORRISON-CARLOCK MINE. Located in Mugginsville, this was one of the largest and most productive mines in the Scott Valley region. (Courtesy Sara Whipple Collection.)

in 1854 on what is now called Whiskey Creek and it was operated by Ensign Smith, who was soon renamed "Whiskey Smith." A story has it that mules headed into Salmon Mountain country often carried a sack of flour on one side, a keg of whiskey on the other.

In Rough and Ready, the Swain brothers built a store and, in 1858, H.B. Bixby built a hotel that was later enlarged. In 1859, the first schools in the area, including those of Rough and Ready, Washington, Douglas, and Franklin, were also established. Competition between the two struggling communities came to a climax when the flood of 1861–1862 destroyed much of Aetna Mills. What residences and businesses were not destroyed were moved to Rough and Ready, including the post office. However, the post office retained the name of Aetna Mills rather than Rough and Ready, creating confusion that persisted for several years.

Crystal Creek (first called Pine Grove), a community just down the road from Etna, was the first to boast a Protestant church in Scott Valley. David H. Lowry was its first lay minister, but "its inspiration came from Rev. Ebenezer Arnold," the superintendent of northern California Methodist churches, who homesteaded in Scott Valley in the spring of 1854. A small log church was built on the Lowry farm, later known as the O.V. Green farm, at what is now called Holzhauser Lane. A number of boys "gathered in with their axes to hew the logs." The Crystal Creek Methodist Church grew rapidly and people came from miles around, often packed to overflowing. A new church was later built on property donated by Lucius S. Wilson. During the Civil War, the church established the Crystal Creek Sanitary Association and assisted in gathering up medical supplies and bandages.

Crystal Creek's primary industry was dairy farming, and the butter and cheese produced by Crystal Creek's farmers was sold all over the area. Henry Cory opened a general store and the Crystal Creek School, organized in 1859, was considered one of the best in the area. Other early residents included Frederich Holzhauser and his family; J. Milton Smith Sr., who directed the Crystal Creek band and orchestra; the Walkers; the Shelleys; O.V. Green's family; and the Wetmores. By 1900, however, Crystal Creek's popularity waned as its population dwindled. Only a stone monument on Highway 3 marks the spot where the small log church was first built.

Oro Fino, meaning "fine gold," located between Quartz and Chapparal Hills, was a bustling mining center until the 1880s, second only to Humbug. In truth, the mining here was considered so rich, claims measured 15 feet by 15 feet rather than 30 feet by 30 feet. Important mines in the Oro Fino region included the Eastlick Mine, Flying Cloud, Oom-Paul, and Blind Lode, to name a few. The first known white man's grave, that of a Hudson Bay trapper, was also discovered here. The school, located about half a mile from the junction of Oro Fino Road and Quartz Valley Road, was established in 1867. Today, nothing of the town remains.

Mugginsville, whose name was supposedly derived from a favorite card game called Muggins, was a thriving community serving miners all over Quartz Valley, including those at the Morrison-Carlock Mine. In 1852, an eight-stamp quartz mill was built on Shackleford Creek nearby. A sawmill was built in 1853 and a grist mill was erected in 1854. Asa Howard, one of Mugginsville's earliest residents, built an inn called the Howard House and a store, and also served as postmaster. In January 1855, his son Scott Howard was born, marking him the second white child born in Scott Valley. (James Parker of Plowman's Valley near Callahan was the first, and Narcissi Davidson is believed to have been the first white girl born in Scott Valley.) In 1860, there were 300 voters polled in the area. Today, only the vacated and deteriorating structure of the Howard House is left.

Greenview was first known as Hayes Corner. A large and stately hotel, the Hayes Hotel was built "up on the hill" in the late 1850s or early 1860s, and it was a popular dance hall and gathering place. Later, the Ford Motor Company of Yreka bought the location and tore the hotel down. A garage was built there that was run by Orin Lewis. The Green family, an early pioneering family, established its residence here and legend has it that the new name evolved from "Green's view." Other businesses established around Greenview included Hughes's Blacksmith, a Denny-Bar store (now the remodeled Senior Nutrition site), the

Siskiyou Creamery, a butcher shop, a theater, and Judge Baldwin's Store and house (later known as the Palmer house). Judge Baldwin was a local circuit judge. Another store, run by Charlie Harris, also served as the post office. Today, Greenview boasts a bank, Mean Gene's Market and gas station, and the Scott Valley Feed Store. The feed store has been operating since the late 1930s, though the original location was in downtown Greenview rather than on State Highway 3. The original business was owned and operated by J.J. and May Burger.

Lesser known mining centers in Scott Valley and along Scott River included the following: French Flat, with a population of 400 men, many Chinese, boasting the first store, saloon, dance hall, and boarding house "all in one building"; Hardscrabble, located about 2 miles below Deadwood; French Bar, located below Scott Bar and abandoned by 1880; and Simonville, located below French Bar and established in 1854. Interestingly, the largest voting precinct in 1856 was the area encircling Scott Bar, French Bar, Simonville, and Johnson's Bar (located between French Bar and Simonville), with 1,500 votes cast.

The Klamath River gold rush came principally in 1852. By that time, 500 to 1,000 miners were working near the junction of the Klamath and Salmon Rivers. Two of the first camps established along the Klamath River included Cottonwood, which was later named Henley and was destroyed by fire in 1861, and Cottage Grove, founded in 1852.

Cottage Grove, located below Swillup Flat, was settled by William and Robert Elliott. They built a house in a small grove of trees and then a store. Others who came during this time and stayed included Abe and Jim Fry (the first postmaster of Cottage Grove in 1857), Henry W. Thomas, John Brown, Raoul Aubrey, and Mr. Alpheus, whose son George remained after he moved on. Most of these early miners married Native American women and reared their families along the river. Because Cottage Grove was located along the Kelsey Trail, Robert Elliott took up packing, a tradition that remained in the family until the early 1920s. The Elliotts also had a sizeable mine that they later developed as a hydraulic mine, employing others as hired hands. Other early mines in this region included the Millikan Bar Mine, the Carter Mine at Blue Nose and the Rood Mine at Rock Creek.

Happy Camp, a community surrounded by mountains and quite isolated even today, supposedly derived its name from a party of miners who, in 1851, celebrated after surviving the arduous journey up the Klamath River. Toasting the spot where the pickings looked good, one miner declared their stopping place to be "a Happy Camp."

Other names associated with Happy Camp's earliest development include Captain Charles McDermitt (the first sheriff of Siskiyou County), the Swain brothers, Captain Gwin Tompkins, Charles D. Moore, J.H. Stinchfield, Jeremiah Martin, Mr. Cochrane, William Bagley, Daniel and Jack McDoughall, William McMahone, Robert Williams, Charles Wilson, John Cox, Charles Southard, George Wood, W.T. Stevens, James Buck, J.W. Burke, Jerry Lane, W.A.J. Moore, William Rumlev, Barney Ray, Mr. Penny, and others. In the late spring or early summer of 1851, these men—many already veterans of mining—took up claims. Only the hardiest remained, braving the rough starvation winter that followed.

It was McDermitt and Tompkins who established the first ferry below the mouth of the Trinity River, known as Blackburn's Ferry. Unfortunately, an attack by Native Americans left three men dead while McDermitt and Tompkins were away in Oregon. As a result of the continued threat of attack, the venture collapsed. After a second assault on miners, where two men were killed and one seriously wounded, the miners gathered together and retaliated against the nearest Indian encampment. Reportedly, all the people found there, including women and children, were killed.

Indian Town, located up Indian Creek, also became a thriving mining camp during the 1850s. In just five years, the community consisted of a bakery and three stores, a bowling alley and a couple saloons, plus a big hotel and butcher shop. In 1856, Indian Town's population jumped to 450 while Happy Camp's population remained around 100. Squire John Prindle was the justice of the peace. Indian Town's bloom didn't last long, though, as miners left when the gold thinned out. However, because it was a main trail leading from Crescent City inland, often called the Waldo Trail (or the Gasquet Trial), it survived for many more years.

HUGHES BLACKSMITH. Jim Hughes operated the first blacksmith shop in Greenview. (Courtesy Hayden Family Collection.)

A second trail, the Kelsey Trail, was cut from Crescent City to Yreka by way of Happy Camp, up the Klamath, across the Marble Mountains, and down Kelsey Creek to Scott River. From Scott River, the trail led to Fort Jones and Yreka. Ferry Point, a small mining camp on the Kelsey Trail, also served the Bunker Hill Mine. For awhile, it prospered and boasted a store, hotel, dance hall, and river ferry. John Titus was an early settler here who fell in love with and married a young Native American woman. Together, they raised 11 children. John eventually made a large strike at Classic Hill Mine on Indian Creek.

As in all parts of Western Siskiyou County, packing remained a principal industry until roads and freight wagons replaced the stalwart mule trains. But as flumes and ditches were built to move water up from the rivers to higher ground for sluicing and hydraulic mining, the demand for lumber quickly grew. In the 1850s, at least two sawmills operated near Happy Camp.

As a result of the rich claims being worked up and down the Klamath River, Happy Camp prospered. By 1860, there were four stores (three run by whites, one by a Chinese man), a hotel, butcher shop, and saloon. There was a brick kiln as well, located on the west bank of Indian Creek. A bridge stretched across Indian

WATER WHEEL. Wheels like this one at a mine near Hamburg were used to generate power used in mills and mining operations. (Courtesy Betty Hall Collection.)

Creek, while the streets nearby were officially named Bridge Street, Main Street, and China Street. As early as 1856, Henry Doolittle owned a hotel called the American House, a home, and a general store. He was also appointed the first Happy Camp postmaster in 1858. Other early businesses in Happy Camp were owned or operated by pioneers James Camp and Company (with James Camp, Heil Camp, and John Titus), Martin Cuddihy, and Albert and Alphonso Doolittle.

Another important community in the Klamath River region was Seiad, originally spelled Sciad. Seiad had been a familiar trapping site before becoming a mining site. Sciad, a Native American name, supposedly means "peaceful valley" or "hole in the ground." The Lowden (or Louden) Ranch, in 1851, was cleared here for an apple orchard. Local miners enthusiastically bought apples for 50¢ each. The Lowden Mine was worked successfully for 35 years, employing many Chinese laborers. Reportedly, $52,000 was removed in one year.

In the 1850s, Hamburg Bar on the Klamath River was a source of good diggings. Nuggets weighing up to 16 ounces were found upriver from Hamburg, at Scott Bar, so miners swarmed to the area that was originally the site of large gatherings of Karuk Indians, according to Henry "Hank" S. Mostovoy. Jimmy Swartz built his sawmill on top of a Native American graveyard located there. It was Sigmund Simon who christened the town Hamburgh, its original spelling in honor of his birthplace in Germany. He raised a flag of flour sacks and red and blue shirts onto a pole. Born in May 1823, Simon came to California by way of Cape Horn. Just 22 years old, he settled first at Scott Bar where he opened a merchandising business.

A second mining town was also named in honor of Simon, called Simonville (near Johnson's Bar), which was settled in 1854. It was here that Simon married Louisa Maria Nentzel, the daughter of his business partner Christopher Nentzel. It was here that the first of their nine children was born as well. Though Simon mined, he was primarily a businessman. When he died in 1881 at age 58, he was the treasurer of the Scott Bar Masonic Lodge No. 108, the Scott River postmaster, and the owner of the Simon and Nentzel Clothing Store in Scott Bar. His widow then became one of the first postmistresses in Siskiyou County.

Another early settler in the Hamburg area was Tom Martin, who came to the area from Ohio in 1851. Tom "bought himself" a Native American bride, Kate Duzel, the daughter of George Adolphus Duzel and "Doc Granny," an herb doctor of the Shasta tribe. As with other miners, intermarriage was common along the river. Together, Tom and Kate had seven children. Sadly, Tom died a wealthy man, having been a successful miner and "one of the first ones to strike amber," but because his wife knew so little of his business affairs, the money was never found. "Grandma Kate" and her children had very little to live on after Tom's death in 1902.

From 1852 until 1859, Hamburg thrived. Some estimates put the population at around 6,000, most being Chinese; at its height, Hamburg boasted three stores, several saloons, a hotel and rooming house, livery stable, freight and passenger stage line stop, and other businesses. The small cemetery dates back to 1860.

One form of mining later developed at Hamburg and other sites along the rivers involved wingdams. A dam, built of lumber or out of willow and small trees, was extended about 75 feet into the river, then turned downstream about 130 feet and back to shore. This formed a large rectangular enclosure out of which all water was pumped, not just once, but continuously (seepage was common). With the water removed, the riverbed lay exposed. Derricks were then installed to hoist out gravel and boulders, leaving the leftover gravel to be shoveled out by hand into sluices. Washed through flumes or sluices, the gold was extracted. Sometimes, water-powered machines called "Chinese pumps" were engineered to remove water from the riverbed. If the water passing through the sluices had to be elevated, water wheels were also constructed; a good flow was required in order to move the sand and gravel across the riffles of the sluice and out the other end. A tedious and convoluted process, wingdams yielded well in many places. The following reference to a wingdam operation appeared in the October 23, 1872 *Yreka Journal*:

> Just below the junction of Scott River, on the Klamath River, Mr. W. Learned is carrying on one of the largest mining operations in that section of country. He has used over 49,000 feet of lumber, and has a flume conveying water from Scott River, carrying about 1,000 inches of water, for the purpose of running two overshot wheels. Altogether, there are four wheels, two overshot and two river wheels, with three pumps in operation, which have a capacity of pumping 100 inches of water each. The derrick is also run by water power, the mast being 60 feet in length and the boom 70 feet, supported by wire guys. Where the wing dam is built, the water in places is 18 feet deep, with a very strong current. He has in his employ about 40 men, who make up quite a mining camp.

This method of diverting the river allowed the miners to dig deeper and deeper. By dipping water out, rock and gravel could be emptied into sluice boxes where gold was removed. Throughout Western Siskiyou County, wingdams were common, especially along the Klamath where the water is deep and moves quickly.

Mining remained the heartbeat of early Siskiyou County through the next few decades. Though changes would soon be made and new industries would evolve, the gold rush established the foundations upon which the rest of the county would be structured.

3. The Civil War and Post–Civil War Eras

For Western Siskiyou County, the period following the gold rush was a time of transition. The hypnotic lure of gold had men rushing off to gold fields opening up in faraway places like the Thompson and Fraser Rivers in British Columbia or the Comstock region of Nevada.

Those who remained turned their sights to new kinds of gold mining, including hard rock mining and hydraulic mining. Hard rock mining requires digging deep into the earth to remove the pay quartz from which gold is extracted through milling or crushing. Tailings, or spent gravel, is what's left behind. Even today, mounds of rock and eroded hillsides provide reminders of the early miners' insatiable quest for gold.

The men who stayed also sent for families. Some, discouraged by not finding their "great strike" or those who wanted to settle down, turned their attention to building businesses or returning to trades they'd pursued in the past. In response to this growth, early trails were widened and improved, as reported in the *Shasta Courier* on June 2, 1857:

> A wagon road is about to be opened to the top of Trinity Mountain. From the summit of Trinity Mountain to Trinity Center, a good road will soon be completed by Mr. Bates and others. From that point to the foot of Scott Mountain, an excellent road has already been made.

A year later, the *Shasta Courier* of June 26, 1858 announced the following:

> The California Stage Company will hereafter run to the top of Trinity Mountain from this side and through Trinity Valley—thus leaving but a short distance to be made on mule back. In a few days, says the *Yreka Union*, stages will be run on the Sacramento to Sweet Water, 10 miles below Soda Springs, thus deducting the mule travel to 30 mules.

ON THE BLUFFS NEAR FORKS. Freight wagons head up the narrow trail along the North Fork of the Salmon River. (Courtesy Siskiyou County Museum.)

By August of 1858, two stage lines ran between Shasta (Redding) and Yreka, one on the Sacramento Route via Shasta Valley, the other through French Gulch across Trinity Mountain, through Scott Valley, and over to Yreka. By 1860, every part of the old trail over Trinity and Scott Mountains had been replaced by a road. On August 10, 1861, the *Sacramento Union* reported the following:

> From Shasta [Redding] to Yreka, a distance of 115 miles, with the exception of about twenty miles through Scott Valley, the road for the whole distance has been made by artificial means, crossing Trinity and Scott Mountains, each at an elevation of nearly three thousand feet above the valleys at their base, by a grade on each mountain that will average six miles up and six miles down. The road through Trinity Valley crosses Trinity River on substantial wooden bridges, with stone abutments as often as fifteen times . . . The whole work cost about seventy thousand dollars. The enterprise of the California Stage Company has been of immense benefit to the people of the northern part of the state and has greatly decreased the cost of transportation and freight and reduced time of travel.

Of course, weather dictated how speedily or how frequently travel took place. In summer, stages could scale Scott Mountain in two hours, but in winter, heavy storms washed out roads, delayed ferries, and halted stages headed north or south.

The winter of 1861–1862 was one of the worst in the county's early history. It began in November of 1861 and, by January 1862, snow lay 15 feet deep on Scott

Mountain, waylaying travelers for three days. High water took out nearly all the bridges between Shasta (Redding) and Weaverville, and Crescent City was almost entirely destroyed. Rain and melting snow raised the Klamath River to 37.5 feet above normal. Yreka Creek overflowed its bank, washing out the bridge and washing away much of the town. Scott River flooded the valley and the entire region became a lake. Bridges, roads, ditches, and mining claims all fell victim to the floods.

Wells recorded, "Klamath River was a raging torrent, the angry waters lashing the sides of their rocky prison and beating themselves into foam in their frenzy." But that was only the beginning. He continued, "A week later, 'the rains descended and the floods came.' [again]" Even the wire bridge spanning the Klamath, "near the mouth of Salmon River, and ninety feet high, although under water, resisted nobly until the logs and driftwood brought down by the flood overcame it, and it went the way of all bridges."

"On Salmon River," Wells notes, "every dam, bridge, mill and flume was washed away or badly damaged, the loss from Sawyer's Bar to the Klamath being estimated at $90,000." Regarding Scott Valley, he wrote the following:

> The river carried everything in its path, including several buildings, while at Etna, the saw-mill went down the stream and the water-wheel of the flour-mill was also borne away . . . The water of Indian Creek forced its way through Hooperville, causing many to abandon their houses and flee for safety, while nearly every vestige of mining operations was obliterated . . . McAdams conquered everything but the Steamboat claim, and, shifting its channel, went tearing through the town of Hardscrabble, at least ten feet deep.

It wasn't enough that the rains came once and then twice, but on December 22, a third storm hit and "swept away what little had been left by its predecessors, and made the universal ruin complete."

But neither the vagaries of weather nor the primitive conditions could deter progress.

Though the approaching Civil War was not felt as keenly in this newly settled region as in the East, a number of Western Siskiyou residents returned to family homes to take up arms. Some of those who had been stationed at Fort Jones also went on to serve in the armies of either the South or North. According to the late Lauran Paine, an award-winning historical author and Scott Valley resident, these included the following:

> Lieutenant Pickett whose immortal Charge at the Battle of Gettysburg marked the tragic end of the great day of the Horse Soldier; William Wing Loring, a Confederate general who, after the Civil War, achieved the highest rank ever held by an American in a foreign army—Pasha and Field Marshall under the Khedive Of Egypt; John B. Hood, the native

Kentuckian who . . . joined the Confederacy . . . and was at the first Union defeat—Bull Run, then helped to drive the Union forces out of Texas in 1862. He was at Gettysburg in 1863 as a Confederate Major General . . . as a Lieutenant General at the Battle of Chickamauga in 1864 he lost his right leg . . . finally, he commanded the defense of Atlanta against Union General William Tecumseh Sherman. There was also Phil Sheridan, who became Army Chief of Staff under President Grant. And there was Grant himself, Absent Without Leave from Fort Jones. And finally, there was Major General George Crook, one of the greatest Union commanders.

Support for the Union in Siskiyou County was overwhelming. A rally and meeting was held at the courthouse on Saturday evening, May 4, 1861, in Yreka, out of which the Yreka Union Club was officially organized. Judge Elijah Steele was elected president; George C. Furber, John S. Peck, and G. Lanphier were co-vice presidents; and C.H. Pollard was elected secretary. Two cannons and a flag were purchased for $100; the cannon were later used at Fourth of July celebrations.

Meanwhile, Siskiyou County's leading semi-weekly newspapers, the *Yreka Union* and the *Journal*, reflected the political divisions facing the nation. The *Yreka Union* was published by H.K. White, a Democrat, while the *Weekly Journal*, once known as the *Northern Journal*, was purchased by Robert Nixon in July 1861. Under his direction, the weekly took up the Republican cause, supporting President Lincoln throughout the war. According to J. Roy Jones, "His [Nixon's] *Journal* became northern California's most potent force in holding California within the Union."

Sam Brannan, so influential in California's early politics, was a candidate for presidential elector on the Union ticket in 1862; he spoke in Yreka on September 21 and in Fort Jones on September 22 at "the greatest meeting ever collected in the Valley."

A company of Siskiyou volunteers was recruited in the summer of 1861 and mustered at Fort Jones on September 11. Company M, Second Cavalry, California Volunteers was led by Captain Charles McDermitt, First Lieutenant George F. Price, and Second Lieutenant Joseph M. Woodworth. The company was placed on the overland trail in Nevada, Utah, and Colorado, keeping settlers safe from Native American attack. McDermitt had earlier served in the Mexican War in 1846. He was also elected first sheriff of Siskiyou County and served in the State Assembly in 1859 and 1860. On August 8, 1865, as lieutenant colonel, McDermitt was killed in a Native American battle in Green River Valley, Nevada.

A second company of volunteers was mustered in under the direction of Deputy Sheriff Joseph "Joe" Smith. Originally designated as a cavalry unit, the men reported to Camp Alert, located southwest of San Francisco, but were told that the cavalry quota was full. The men marched out of camp, then took the river steamer to Sacramento at their own expense to enlist in the newly formed Fifth

Regiment Infantry. With 60 of the original 80 present, they were designated the first company, or Company A. In June 1862, Company A, still under the leadership of Captain Joe Smith, marched to Fort Buchanan in southern Arizona.

According to Colonel J. Marius Scammell in the 1960 *Siskiyou Pioneer*, the Fifth Infantry "ultimately became part of the 'The Column from California' that occupied Nevada, served in New Mexico (and a part of Texas), and which made prodigious marches over a desert country (sometimes 36, 40, or even 53 miles a day) with only one meal a day and a couple of hours of rest. The heat and dust were insupportable to all except hardy men." The October 29, 1862 *Yreka Journal* likewise reported that the *Chicago Times* had written regarding the Fifth Infantry that "those troops have set an example to our Northern soldiers which should not pass unheeded."

In April 1863, Company A was attacked by 50 to 60 Apaches, a skirmish that left six Native Americans dead as well as Private William Hussey of Yreka. Sergeant Thomas Sittan of Scott River was wounded and later cited for gallantry. In June, Private Justus B. Wagoner of Yreka and Private John Hinkley of Alleghany were

CHARLES McDERMITT. This soldier and early settler in Scott Valley was killed in action in Arizona. (Courtesy Fort Jones Museum.)

killed by Native Americans while carrying dispatches to Santa Fe. (Wagoner's family had been killed by Rogue River Indians in 1854 and 1855.) The company also saw action in July 1864, while scouting for Apaches on the Rio San Francisco. Company A was eventually mustered out on November 30, 1864 at La Mesilla, New Mexico; Major Smith mustered out in April 1865. In all, four members were killed in action or died of wounds, and one member was lost to desertion.

A third group, Company D, Fifth Brigade, Siskiyou Light Guard was formed in June 1863, and a Scott Valley guard, Company F, Fifth Brigade, under Captain Robert Baird, mustered in 67 men in January 1864. Their purpose was to fight hostile Native Americans in Humboldt County. Headquartered in Fort Jones, they served actively until mustered out in June 1865.

Another endeavor residents of Siskiyou County took up during the course of the war was in relief efforts. The Yreka Sanitary Commission, organized on

PETER LIGHTHILL. This member of a pioneering family served in the Union Army during the Civil War. (Courtesy Fort Jones Museum.)

September 1, 1862, collected donations. Under the direction of William Irwin, president; Dr. E. Wadsworth, secretary-treasurer; M. Sleeper; C.E. Burrows; Jerome Churchill; John Colby; and Henry Fried, $6,000 was collected and forwarded to San Francisco in less than a month. The town of Simonville sent $125 in February 1863. Branches of the relief association sprung up all over Western Siskiyou County, the first ones in Deadwood, with 63 members, and Scott Bar, with 100 members. Oro Fino organized a branch with 78 members. Humbug formed an association with 25 members. Fort Jones had 71 and Crystal Creek had 79 members.

In addition, the Ladies' Yreka Lint Association was organized in October 1862, under Mrs. F.S. Farren as president and Mrs. J.S. Feelows and Mrs. M.J. Bradley as vice presidents. Weekly meetings were held to prepare rolls of bandages and scrap lint. The clothing, lint, bandages, and supplies were then forwarded to battlefront hospitals by Wells, Fargo and Company "free of charge."

One local ardent Southern sympathizer was G.L. Greathouse. A banker, he bought up controlling interest in the "Big Ditch"—the enormous ditch that miners working Yreka Flats had built to transport water. As the war took shape, Greathouse privately funded and outfitted a couple of frigates for the Confederate navy, spending considerable money on the endeavor and angering many around Yreka. In 1862 and 1863, after a series of severe winter storms damaged whole sections of the ditch, Greathouse was forced to borrow $30,000 to cover repairs. The cost was so great that he, in turn, was forced to sell his interest in the ditch company.

A few of those who took up arms during the Civil War included Dr. Francis Sorrell, a local physician who had been elected assemblyman of the district in November 1860, but relinquished his office to serve the Confederacy. By December 1861, he was a surgeon in Richmond, Virginia. Southern sympathizer Edward Stallcup, who did not migrate to Siskiyou County until after the war, first served with the Texas Rangers, then as a cavalryman under General Lee. Stallcup became a prominent citizen in the Big Springs area southeast of Yreka. Dr. J.W. Reins also served in the Confederate army as a surgeon, then came to Yreka and Etna after the war.

Joseph Herbert served in the Illinois 36th regiment. He also worked as a packer while in the Klondike gold fields before coming to Scott Bar as a miner. Leon Sovey fought for the Union army before coming to Scott Valley with his young wife, Mary. Mary Sovey later became something of a midwife and nurse. E.E. Williams, "who was twice wounded in battle and once narrowly escaped being taken prisoner when his company was forced to retreat after exhausting their ammunition," later married Mary Crooker and settled in Scott Bar.

John Franklin Boyle was a Siskiyou County pioneer and mining engineer who fought in the war before coming west. At 15 years of age, he ran away from home and joined the Union navy. He served as a messenger boy to the captain of a gunboat and was on gunboat patrol on the Potomac River searching for J.W. Booth at the time of Lincoln's assassination. After the war, he traveled overland

and became one of Siskiyou County's first consulting mining engineers. He once stated that he "was in the Union forces on one side of the Potomac River, while the late Robert Rankin was on the other side with the Confederate forces."

Jacob Conner, great-great-great-grandfather to Greg Lindholm of Greenview, came to Deadwood to prospect in 1850, then left California to join the Union army. After the war, he married Constantia Douglas Stephens in Hancock County, Illinois, before returning to Siskiyou County. Jacob again took up mining, this time filing for a claim in Oro Fino at what would be called the Fletcher-Wright Mine.

Michael Lighthill also joined the fight for the North. He enlisted in the 17th Kentucky Infantry (Company A) and fought in several major battles, including the Siege of Vicksburg. Jacob Eller, who served in the 34th Iowa Regiment, fought at the Battle of Vicksburg. He, his wife, and their children came to Scott Valley in 1874. Harve Vanderpool, Bernita Tickner's great-grandfather, was also a Civil War veteran who fought for the Union. He was wounded in one eye, an injury that plagued him many years later. Peter Lighthill likewise fought for the North.

Lucius Fairchild and his brother Cassius both entered the Civil War. Lucius had been a butcher with several stores in Scott Bar prior to returning home to Wisconsin. He had also been a partner with Elijah Steele in a mining claim. When war broke out, he immediately joined up as captain of Company K of the First Wisconsin Volunteers. He became colonel of the Second Wisconsin, part of the famous Iron Brigade, and general when he led the counter-attack against General George Pickett at Gettysburg. In the battle, Lucius lost his arm. His brother was killed. After the war, Lucius Fairchild went on to become secretary of state and governor, three terms in a row. He also served the United States as a consul overseas. He died in 1896 at 65 years of age.

Celebrations were frequently held around Siskiyou County in tribute to Union victories. After Charleston's capture by the North, Yreka celebrated by firing 36 guns. And with Richmond's capture, the *Weekly Journal* reported "great rejoicing among the Union men in parts of the country. In Yreka one hundred guns were fired on the plaza. Copperheads feel disagreeable." Again, on April 6, a torch light procession was held, the parade "stopping at intervals to fire a six-pound artillery piece." General Lee's surrender was announced "from the pulpit of the M.E. [Methodist-Episcopal] Church by Rev. A.C. McDougall. There was no restraining the congregation's enthusiasm." A parade was held the next day; an effigy of Jefferson Davis was suspended from a "tree" and 100 guns were fired in tribute.

News of Lincoln's assassination reached Yreka and the surrounding towns on April 15. Within minutes, businesses were closed and flags hung at half-mast. Services were held all over the county and, for days, people flocked to their churches to hear sermons and mourn for the dead president. On April 20, funeral ceremonies were held in Yreka and William Irwin led a somber procession through town to the pavilion on North Street where L.M. Ketcham delivered a eulogy.

One of the biggest problems that faced California and Western Siskiyou County after the war was the 1 million ex-soldiers who had to re-enter civilian life. At the same time, immigrants were arriving in increasing numbers, from approximately 250,000 to 460,000 in 1873. A post-war depression in 1866 and 1867 also left eastern industries with an abundance of workers, so the influx of humanity had no place to go but west. The government responded by offering land to settlers; the offer was made even more appealing after construction of the Union Pacific Railroad was complete.

Communication in all its forms was important to Western Siskiyou County. Whereas the first telegraph line in California was completed in September 1853, it wasn't until January of 1858 that the first telegraph message was sent from Red Bluff to Shasta. Furthermore, the Northern California Telegraph Company didn't arrive in Yreka until July of 1858. Lines were laid over Trinity and Scott Mountains, through Scott Valley, and along McAdams, Cherry, and Greenhorn Creeks. On August 5, 1858, the *Sacramento Union* declared, "The *Yreka Union* was issued at 11 o'clock last night containing the first telegraphic dispatches from Marysville, Sacramento and San Francisco."

On October 24, 1861, the first through message by telegraph was sent to President Lincoln from Stephen J. Fields, chief justice of California—after 1,600 miles of wire were laid in four months. The cost to send a wire was $7.75 for ten words from San Francisco to New York, plus an additional $2 from Yreka. Extra

WAGON ON SALMON MOUNTAIN. These freight wagons are pulling up to the summit of Salmon Mountain. (Courtesy McBroom Family Collection.)

words cost from 45¢ to 60¢, plus an additional 75¢ for each additional five words out of Yreka. Siskiyou County's first local telegraph office was installed in Yreka at Autenrieth's Drug Store, then moved to Parker's Book Store. Sometime during the Civil War, the Northern California Telegraph Company was sold to the Western Union Company.

Seventeen years later, it was E.H. Autenrieth who sent away for the first telephone apparatus and, on Sunday, December 8, 1878, he and George Peck set up a connection from Yreka to Jacksonville, Oregon (60 miles away). People crowded into the telegraph office to watch and listen to the new-fangled contraption. At either end, cornets played and people sang; "Miss Etta Sleeper and A.E. Raynes favored Jacksonville with several songs, perhaps rendering a recent song-hit, 'The Little Spring Beside My Cabin Home.' "

The Pony Express, which ran from St. Joseph, Missouri to Placerville, California, started on April 3, 1860, lasting approximately two years. Before this time, mail arrived only monthly. As roads improved, however, stage and freight lines assisted packers in hauling mail in and out of the isolated mountain communities, a business that lasted well into the twentieth century.

To keep stage routes open, oxen were often quartered at the base of Scott Mountain for use during heavy snows. The following was reported on December 27, 1867 in the *Yreka Journal*:

OVER THE MOUNTAIN. Ahlgren and a mule head up the trail in deep snow. Note the snow shoes on the mule. (Courtesy McBroom Family Collection.)

There is from 12 to 15 feet of snow on Scott Mountain which is completely blocked with snow. They have oxen at work opening the road on south side. Trinity valley has from four to five feet of snow and oxen will soon have it open to travel. The telegraph is open over the Scott mountain, as far as the New York House and will soon be open to Shasta (Redding).

The *Shasta Courier* of January 11, 1868 wrote, "The Trinity Center Stage driver informs that a heavy fall of snow has occurred on Trinity and Scott mountains the past few days and the roads are in horrible condition . . . Passengers and mail are being transported over Scott mountain in sleighs."

Mail had to be carried in by horseback from Yreka to Oak Bar and beyond. Gold dust made up the loads headed out to Yreka, but mail—and whiskey—were packed back in. Five-gallon kegs of whiskey were loaded, one on each side of a mule, and the rest of the load went on top. Supplies often hauled to the miners downriver included overalls and chewing tobacco. Chester Barton's father, while still in his teens, packed mail from Yreka to Oak Bar, two trips a week, two days over and back. He also packed mail to Scott Bar and back. Later, he drove a Concord stage and also did the following:

> He took the first four-horse stage into Happy Camp . . . That was before any road over Cade Mountain. The road went over from Grider Creek to China Creek and then you crossed on either the Evans or the Gordon ferry . . . Then he went around Cade Mountain into Happy Camp from there. Dave Cudahy had the saloon and hotel in Happy Camp.

The earliest built stages were the "thorough-brace" type, as they were built to withstand rough roads, supported as they were by heavy leather straps of several thicknesses. Mud wagons were also used, though they were not as comfortable as the larger thorough-brace stages.

The Concord stage was a heavier and larger coach drawn by four or six horses. It held nine passengers, accommodating ten or twelve more on top and two alongside the driver. There was a leather-covered "boot" for carrying mail and baggage. In 1883, L. Swan of Yreka built half a dozen new stages; iron work was done by blacksmith P.O. LeMay, the upholstery was done by Fred Ringe, and Jake Martin painted. Wagon making continued to be a lucrative business in Siskiyou County until after the turn of the century.

Driving freight wagons or stages was dangerous, but it was a critically important occupation in Western Siskiyou County. Drivers and teamsters were held in high regard by everyone and quickly became local heroes. According to J. Roy Jones, some of Siskiyou County's most colorful "jehus," or drivers, included Dan Cawley, Al and Hank Giddings, W.L. Smith, Charlie Laird, Dan Haskel, Joe Bacon, John Mack, and Frank Hovey. One tragic stage incident occurred in 1870 when Jerry Woods drowned after his stage overturned in "a swift running creek

61

between Fort Jones and Callahan's Ranch. The four horses he was driving were also drowned, but the passengers escaped."

Frank Lloyd, a popular and experienced teamster and driver in the 1870s and 1880s, felt fortunate to have never been held up, though he came close. Marcus Isaacs was another well-known teamster in Etna. Kate McCauley, who drove the Klamath River road, was referred to as the "Annie Oakely of the Klamath." Marcus Isaacs was another early teamster who became postmaster of Etna and later opened a small variety store. He married Mary Young from Gazelle.

In the 1870s, Johnny Harris created a stir when he successfully carried mail over snow-packed Salmon Mountain, taking it on his back while he rode skis (or snowshoes, as they were called then). In 1892, he and his brother were awarded the first contract to haul mail over on the new wagon road from Etna to Sawyer's Bar.

The two men purchased two Concord coaches and eight span of horses. Johnny and Edward Harris were so well trusted that they often "acted as purchasing agents for dress materials and shoes as well as fresh meat and vegetables for the housewives." When Johnny wasn't driving the Salmon Mountain summit road, he drove stage between Etna and Yreka. Johnny and Edward Harris also founded the Taylor Lake Mine in 1903.

Throughout the Civil War and post-war period, mining remained strong, though surface gold was playing out and new methods of mining were being introduced, particularly deep mining (quartz mining) and hydraulic mining. In 1861, Klamath River mines prospered. At Indian Creek, a rich quartz lead was discovered by McKinley and Company. Blue Bar, on Indian Creek, reportedly paid out $20 a day to each hand, while Doolittle's mine at Happy Camp paid $15. Above Happy Camp, Church and Company wing-dammed the river and paid out $10 a hand. Simonville, one of the most important mining locations along the Klamath, included mines operated by Andrews, Baxter and Company and Joseph Ramus.

In 1877, James Camp and Company patented the claims that became the Classic Hill Mine, one of the larger producers in the Happy Camp region. Other mining interests they held included sites at Clear Creek, Wingate, Elk Creek, Grider and Curley Jack Creeks, George Wood's Bar, and Muck-a-Muck Flat. But being civic-minded, the company also built a steel and wood bridge across Indian Creek in 1883. Gus Meamber was commissioned to haul the steel down to Happy Camp. According to Bill Mathews Sr., "One great feat of Gus's packing was taking some long irons into Happy Camp . . . They were so long they had to be packed on the side of mules at each end of the iron, so the mules were in pairs with irons on both sides. They had men and boys lead each mule so they could make some short turns without shoving each other over the dangerous bluffs." The bridge was later sold to Del Norte County.

Horace Gasquet, another Happy Camp pioneer and entrepreneur, opened stores in Happy Camp and Gasquet in California, and Waldo in Oregon. To keep his stores stocked, he also ran pack trains from the coast. In 1877, he bought the holdings of the Happy Camp Hydraulic Mining Company, which he then sold to a New York buyer.

S.S. Richardson's Mine, later named the Richardson Bedrock Mine, was a large producer that operated for many years. It employed dozens of Chinese laborers and constructed the ditch and flume that transported water from Elk Creek.

The Black Bear Quartz Mine, situated near the head of Black Bear Creek, a tributary of the South Fork of the Salmon River, was discovered in 1860 by M.M. Hart. The road constructed to connect the mine and mill was the first one built in Salmon River country. In 1862, the Union Company, under Ned Roberts, was formed after he discovered a large quartz vein at Eddy's Gulch on the Salmon River.

This kind of mining was deep mining and required ore to be brought up to the surface and crushed. In order to handle larger amounts of ore, however, specialized machinery was needed. One such device was the arrastra, which can be described as follows:

BLACK BEAR MINE. This mine on the Salmon River was one of the most productive in the region. (Courtesy Siskiyou County Museum.)

a shallow, stone-lined pit with a post set in the center [sometimes a tree, cut off at the desired height, was used as the center post]. A horizontal crossbeam was attached to the center post so that it could turn. One or more large stones, called "drags" or "mullers", were placed in the pit and were attached to the crossbeam by ropes or chains. The ore, broken into small fragments, was thrown into the pit along with some water, and as the cross-beam was turned around, the rock was crushed.

The Commodore Mine, located on Barkhouse Creek, Oak Bar, was discovered by C.S. Humphrey and W.H. Quigley in 1894. The mine actually included five claims, with an arrastra built a mile down on the main creek. The yield averaged $17 per ton.

Stamp mills were used for large-scale operations. More expensive and complicated than the arrastra, they were used to process greater quantities of quartz. The stamp mill became the most popular machine used to mill quartz in Siskiyou County; in 1898, there were 70 mills operating. Of those, 48 were water-powered, 15 were steam-powered, and 3 were powered by a combination of steam and water (what powered the remaining 4 is not known).

CHINESE SERVANT. This servant stands beside John Daggett's chair at Daggett's home at the Black Bear Mine. (Courtesy Siskiyou County Museum.)

JOHN DAGGET. Seated here atop his horse on a snowy day, Daggett went on to serve as lieutenant governor of California and superintendent of the mint at San Francisco. (Courtesy Siskiyou County Museum.)

Some of the larger operations included Black Bear, the Gold Run, the old Ball Mines on the Salmon River, and the Klamath Mine at the head of Eddy's Gulch. The Morrison-Carlock Gold Mine in Mugginsville, with a ten-stamp mill, produced more than $200,000 in its first three years of operation and, by 1904, had grossed $470,000 total. This mine also had the longest chute of any Siskiyou County mine, at 1,600 feet. The *Yreka Journal*, on June 18, 1873, described operations at the Klamath Mine:

> They have run four tunnels with an aggregate of 460 feet. The incline from the mine to the mill is 3,100 feet, with 500 feet additional to be added . . . Quartz is run down in five minutes from mine to mill, with perfect safety. 100 tons a day can be sent down in this manner . . . The mill is 58 feet wide and 120 feet long . . . The mill has 32 stamps, and is capable of crushing from 45 to 50 tons per day . . . At present 56 men are employed at the mine.

A promising quartz lead was found on Humbug and, by 1863, Dakin and Company had a ten-stamp mill going with two more planned. The quartz vein,

120 feet deep and 2 feet wide, yielded $400 to $500 a ton. By 1864, however, most activity was only along the forks from Frenchtown (once called Mowry's Flat, but renamed because of the number of French men who mined there) to Harvey's on North Fork.

Many of the laborers sought for use in these large mines were, of course, the Chinese. They would work long hours for less pay. As a result, immigration soared in post-war California and, during the 1870s, the number of Chinese coming to Siskiyou County increased by almost two-thirds. With such an increase in population, resentment also grew, and the movement of the Chinese was noted in newspapers all over California. A few Republican papers, like the *Yreka Journal* and the *Union*, were only moderately opposed to the presence of Chinese, while other, radical Republican newspapers statewide and nationally promoted equality and citizenship for Chinese immigrants.

In contrast, the Democratic *Yreka Union* scoffed at these radicals' tabloids, remarking that they were "all in gushing sympathies for 'John' (the nickname given to the Chinese)." In 1870, the *Yreka Union* declared that the attempt to grant Chinese any citizenship privileges was "the crowning stroke of infamy, to seek to place on an equality with Christian freemen, these filthy spawn of Asia with the leprosy taint of centuries in their veins." Moreover, " 'John' is likely to usurp in the future, not only the place 'Pat' and 'Hans' and other poor white trash, but of 'Sambo' as well."

Even Bret Harte, who considered himself sympathetic to Chinese rights, provided ammunition against the Chinese. His poem "Plain Language from Truthful James" stereotyped the caricature of the Chinese as clever and dishonest, a stereotype used over and over again in the local press. Ironically, when President Hayes and General Sherman visited Yreka in 1880, the town was lit by dozens of Chinese lanterns and the ever-popular Chinese fireworks were used in celebrating the Fourth of July and New Year's.

There were occasional problems between the Native Americans and Chinese as well. On August 14, 1862, a pack train, run by Chinese, was headed down Plummer Creek. A raiding party attacked the train, killing everyone except one white man, who hid in the rocks. This raiding party had earlier made a raid on George Green Brown, burning a barn and driving off 30 head of cattle.

Clearly, prejudice against Native Americans and against Chinese, Mexicans, and others by whites increased during the post-war period. Judge Elijah Steele, who had arrived in California early in 1850, was appointed Indian Agent for northern California by President Lincoln on August 10, 1863. In early February 1864, he held a meeting with heads of several local Native American tribes and, as a result, a peace treaty was drawn up. According to J. Roy Jones, the treaty was signed by Schonchin and the La Lakes, and other chiefs of the Modoc and Klamath River, by John and Jim of the Scott Valley and Humbug, and by Josh and Jack of the Shastas.

Additionally, "intertribal warfare and theft, an agreed friendship with the white men, and negroes and Chinamen living under the white man's laws, right of

BLACK BEAR MINERS. *Black Bear Mine was worked by 300 miners, including dozens of Welsh and Chinese. (Courtesy Siskiyou County Museum.)*

trespass, together with many other grievances, one with the other, were included in the agreement, and signed."

In spite of the prejudice, however, more and more immigrants came to work in the mines or opened their own business. A number of South Islanders, called Kanakas, arrived in Siskiyou County in the 1860s and settled along the Klamath River. Today, only a sign identifies the site of the Honolulu School, built in 1890 in honor of these early immigrants. It has been suggested that the Kanakas were originally shanghaied and brought to San Francisco, then escaped and made their way north. In 1933, on one of his fishing expeditions down the Klamath River, President Hoover visited the school, commenting on the hot lunch program, a soup kettle operation organized and directed by Mrs. Elsie Freeman DeAvilla, a teacher who spent more than 30 years in the district.

However, in time, many gold claims were sold to Chinese miners, even though friction continued. Taxes were imposed on the Chinese who mined, but many fared well anyway. Rather than spending their money, however, they shipped it back to China. More than $50,000 worth of gold dust was sent back to China in 1867 alone. Of course, this added to the belief that the Chinese were interlopers who did not contribute to the local economy. In spite of this, several Chinese, American, and Portuguese mining companies worked side by side in reasonable harmony.

HAPPY CAMP STORE. Jim Kong owned this popular store c. 1915. From left to right are (front row) Frank Murrie, Jim Kong, and Mike Effman; (back row) John Attebery, Ray Storrs, Frank Collins, Cody Attebery, and John Effman. (Courtesy Siskiyou County Museum.)

In Happy Camp, *c.* 1860, there were four stores (three for white and one Chinese). The China Store was owned by Ah Ock, who also owned mines and employed his own laborers. All four stores were supplied by the China Bow Pack Train. A second Chinese store, owned by the Kong brothers, was famous for its Chinese candy and Chinese whiskey. By 1880, Happy Camp's Chinese population rose to 250 (out of a total population of 597 miners); its Native American population was numbered at 97.

Joseph Reeves owned large mines around Happy Camp and Seiad and employed many Chinese. One mine, named China Creek, was sold to Chinese miners who successfully removed $200,000—a considerable sum for a relatively small operation.

In truth, there were hundreds of mines operated by Chinese miners. Most, as with mines worked by white miners, never earned a name, but some came to be recognized by locals over time. Some of the mines in Western Siskiyou County that were either sold or operated by Chinese miners included the Owens mine on Indian Creek where, in the 1880s, Charles Owen paid over $4,000 for a tunnel they constructed; the Richardson hydraulic claim, which produced about $50,000 each month, or upwards of $1,000 a day; the Classic Hill Mine on Indian Creek, which was leased to a number of Chinese in the 1880s and allegedly removed more than $1 million in gold; the Muck-a-Muck (or Minnie Reeves Mine), which yielded more than $75,000 a year; and the Lowden Mine, which was estimated to have cleaned up $52,000 in one year. Near Seiad was the Masonic Bar Mine, which was operated by Chinese with derricks using water from Grider Creek. Across from the Portuguese Mine was the Hoskins Bar Mine, also operated by Chinese using a dip wheel. At the mouth of Scott River was a Chinese mine at Johnson Bar, while another one was located further up at Beebe Bar (or Michigan Bar).

According to Edward Leduc, in his "Memories of Scott Bar" in the *1978 Siskiyou Pioneer*, the Chinatown at Scott Bar included several houses, a rooming house and a Joss house. He recalled the following:

> The kids [in Scott Bar] went to China Town during the period of Chinese New Year because the Chinese passed out small bags of Chinese candy. I remember the sugar-covered coconut strips, pieces of ginger candy and some Chinese nuts, one of which was about 3/4" in diameter with a soft shell and inside was a pit covered with fruit about the size of a small plum (called a Liechee nut) . . . With the possible exception of one man who was a cook at the Eagle Hotel, the last of the Chinese left Scott Bar in 1907. I know because six of them came to work for my brother-in-law, Joe Martin, at the Bailey Mine below Seiad. After a few months they left but I do not know where they went.

A small Chinese population lived in Etna, "down off China Hill." According to Bernice Tickner, Etna historian, there were 11 homes located there, as well as a red-light district. After many of the mines played out, the Chinese took employment as ranch hands and servants. One or two owned stores, including China Yum, who owned a restaurant. Only two Chinese women lived in the Etna community: Chinee Mary and Old Susie. Because they dressed in trousers, they were a curiosity. Eventually, Chinee Mary moved to Yreka and, from there, she returned to China.

Sadly, the 1880s were a time of extreme racism, not only in Siskiyou County, but also around the state and nation. In 1882, the Exclusion Acts were passed and other more restrictive measures approved. In 1888, the Scott Bill excluded at least 20,000 Chinese from returning to the states after leaving temporarily to go home. And wherever the Chinese went, they were harassed or taunted.

Fires devastated several Chinatowns around the county, like the fires of 1856 and 1871 in Yreka. A smaller one occurred in 1878, followed by a bigger fire in August 1886. From Miner Street to Lane Street, and from Center Street to Yreka Creek, the fire raged. Not only was Chinatown destroyed, other businesses, including the J.B. Marble Works, an undertaker's parlor, and Martin's Paint Store on Main Street were charred. As a result, the new Chinatown was moved across Yreka Street to where it would not pose a threat to the rest of the town. Happy Camp's Chinatown also burned in 1910, after which most of the residents left. In fact, by the early 1920s, only two Chinese men lived in Happy Camp; both worked for Miss Minnie Reeve as ranch hands.

In spite of the political and social climate, mining in Siskiyou County prospered after the Civil War. By 1870, quartz mining was in full swing and, by 1900, more than 110 quartz mines were still operating. Some of the mines being worked in the Salmon River area included the Know Nothing Mine, King Solomon's Mine at the head of Mathews Creek, the Morning Star Mine at the head of Jackass Creek, the Mulloy Mine at Tanner's Peak at the head of Rattlesnake Creek, the Live Yankee Mine, the Evening Star, and the Victory Mine, worked by John Pephroney.

The famous Black Bear, considered one of the finest quartz mills in the state, was in full operation by the middle of September 1862. In 1863, John Daggett and Alfred Cave reported to the State Mining Bureau that the Salmon River had yielded more than $20 million in gold. In 1865, Daggett, John Coughlan, and John Reid bought out Hart and his partners and built a 16-stamp mill.

Some of the first mining machinery had to be packed in by mule train from the coast, but some was brought up the lower Klamath River canyon by Native American women carrying large burden baskets. Deacon Lee hauled equipment in ox carts from Callahan, up the Scott River, and over to Eddy's Gulch, then around to Black Bear. To navigate the steep slopes, the wheel on the upper side of the cart was small, while the wheel on the lower side was big. This kept the cart even as man and animal traversed the hillsides.

A school was built at Black Bear in 1869 as the payroll climbed to 300 men, plus their families. A large number of experienced Cornish miners had been brought in to work the mine. Next, Chinese were hired, an act which reportedly made many miners angry. While Daggett was away in San Francisco, the following is reported to have happened:

> . . . hot-headed Irishmen dragged one of the Chinese men down through town, killing him. In response, Mrs. Daggett sent her son off with a wire for Mr. Daggett, telling him to return home. When the boy went to meet his father on the appropriate stage, a gunfighter, instead of Mr. Daggett, stepped down. The gunfighter went to the saloon where the Irishmen began harassing him. The bartender, cautioning the miner, said, "You better leave him alone. He just cleaned out Bodie." There were no more problems at Daggett's mine.

When Daggett and company sold the mine in 1872 to a group of San Francisco capitalists, the mine was yielding $10,000 a month. The mill was then expanded to a 32-stamp mill, run by both water and steam, and operated successfully for more than ten years. In 1885, when the mine came up for sale, Daggett, convinced the operation was still profitable, repurchased controlling rights in the Black Bear Mine. Entrepreneur and politician, he also served as lieutenant governor of the state of California and as superintendent of the San Francisco Mint.

One of the best mines ever discovered on the Scott River (South Fork) was the Montezuma Mine. The mine started just above Callahan's Ranch. Alexander Parker was one of the owners and Jim Parker was the manager. At some point, the Montezuma was sold to the China Company at South Fork for $50,000, but the South Fork continued to yield. More than 400 pocket miners and somewhere between 500 and 800 Chinese moved over from Coffee Creek and other locations. The big China Mine was just downriver from South Fork. Another mine in the region, near the mouth of Fox Creek, was the ABC Mine, owned by Andrews, Beroy, and Coggins. This mine was later sold to the French Company and run by Alexis Bouvier.

From 1872 to 1885, gold continued to be extracted along the Klamath River, from Humbug to the Scott River. The average amount of gold taken equaled $1.39 per cubic yard. Claims such as the Maplesden Wingdam, below McKinney Creek, yielded $30,000. The Oak Bar-Kleaver and Portugese Company Mine yielded $60,000, while the Centennial Mine, above Lum Grey Mott and Company, yielded $97,000. The Spengler Mine, at the mouth of Humbug Creek, eventually yielded $234,858, and the Mott Company Mine at Manzanita Bar yielded $300,000. Records show that William Kleaver and Company took out, with 11 men, 1 derrick, and hand shoveling, 48 ounces, or $804, in one day. The Portuguese Company, after 3 days and with 11 men and one derrick, removed $3,000 at Oak Bar.

HYDRAULIC MINING. *This operation on the Salmon River features a pole derrick for removing rocks. (Courtesy Siskiyou County Museum.)*

Hydraulic mining was another popular form of gold extraction, primarily during the winter and spring months when water was high. Though developed as early as 1852, it was not used commonly in Siskiyou County until several years later, but, by 1900, it outnumbered all other forms of mining. In fact, the 1898 Register of Mines and Minerals listed 229 hydraulic mines in Siskiyou County, while it listed only 41 drift mines and 101 ground-sluicing mines. Only a few wingdam operations were listed.

The process of hydraulic mining involved channeling a large stream of water through a narrow pipe, called "giants," so that it washed away the hillsides where a vein had been located. Large sluice boxes, not unlike those used in placer mining, were placed in strategic locations so that the dirt and gravel were slushed through. Sometimes, trenches were constructed to carry the material to the sluices or men with wheelbarrows moved the dirt. Rocks and boulders too large to sluice were hauled away or lifted out by derricks. Of course, this kind of mining destroyed or altered much of the landscape.

Some hydraulic mines grew to gigantic proportions. Extensive systems of flumes and sluices had to be constructed for moving water and material. Water, channeled through pipe up to 22 inches in diameter, cascaded down from 500 feet and washed enormous quantities of dirt and material away. Some giants could shoot water more than 200 feet. Sometimes, two giants were at work at the same

HYDRAULIC MINING. Sometimes dangerous, the substantial profits from hydraulic mining were worth the risk because the method was efficient and relatively inexpensive. (Courtesy Siskiyou County Museum.)

time. Many miners were able to rework old placer deposits by switching to hydraulic mining.

One hydraulic mine, near Yreka Flats and worked by a group of Chinese miners, yielded $500 a week. Sometimes the finer gold was washed away, though, so an "undercurrent" or separate, gentler sluice was set up to catch it. At Grider Creek, miners could work all year, as the water level remained high enough. And deeper pits required hydraulic elevators to lift the gravel back up to the level of the sluices.

The Van Bruant Mine (Happy Camp Mine) was one of the largest hydraulic mines in northern California, extending 2 miles in length. Water for the mine came from Indian Creek and, because there was a large water supply, it could run all year. Today, the Happy Camp airport sits on the old mine site.

The Oro Fino Mine, owned by the Eastlick family, was another of the larger hydraulic operations in Western Siskiyou County. In fact, the Oro Fino mining region was second only to Humbug in gold production. And when the pay dirt went so deep that it couldn't be drained of excess water and tailings, mine owner Lafe Eastlick devised what would become known as the "hydraulic elevator." As noted in the *1957 Siskiyou Pioneer*, "Lafe Eastlick's invention opened a new era in mining, that of sub-surface hydraulic mines."

W.P. Bennett had seven hydraulic mines, including the Forks of Salmon River Mining Company, the Never Sweat, Nigger Hill, the Crapo, Knutson, and Horn Mines. Water was brought out of Big Creek on the North Fork of the Salmon and a flume was built straight down between the two rivers. P.C. and Nels Lange had a hydraulic mine on Barkhouse Creek around 1888.

But mining was no longer the only industry being developed. Beginning in the early 1850s, there were already a few established ranches and farms. Miners needed food and many of the disenchanted settled down to start businesses. In a short time, agriculture in and around Western Siskiyou County began to flourish. Potatoes were planted on Salmon River's North Fork in 1855 and proved successful. The first crop of any size, however, was hay, and, in short order, rolled barley, wheat, and oats were grown. In 1878, as reported by Reichman and Reynolds for the Fort Jones wheat and flour market, "No. 1 choice wheat is selling for 75 cents per bushel, oats 50 cents per bushel."

Dairy products were in constant demand, so small creameries were established on farms and ranches throughout the region. As author Brian Helsaple writes, "The real gold that was used to make land payments, 'butter.' . . . The $2.00 or more per pound price that butter fetched in the 1800s went an awful lot further than it does today." Hayden, in his book *Along our History's Trail*, explained how butter was stored or transported. First, it was made into 2-pound rolls, then into blocks. It was packed into 5-pound round tins and larger for hotel or boarding houses, or packed in brine in sealed metal cases.

The Siskiyou County Agricultural Society designed the plans for a Yreka fairgrounds and the first county fair was held in October 1867. Earlier fairs had been held in Scott Valley, the first as early as the late 1850s.

Orchards were also planted and a few vineyards, and whoever could grow a garden did so. Apples were pressed into cider, dried for winter, or stored in root cellars. Hogs, many of which were turned out into the hills where they multiplied quickly, were butchered and turned into ham, sausage, and bacon, meat products easily stored over winter. Especially in Scott Valley, farmers enjoyed increasing sales of their produce and livestock. Cattle were turned out on mountain ranges in the summer months to graze on the abundant meadow grasses, then brought home to winter in the valleys each fall. Harry H. Green, in his *Fort Jones Semi-Centenary*, recalled watching Horace Mitchell as he passed through town with "a band of cattle from David Horn's Klamath River range, bound for the Black Bear mines. Mr. Horn has a contract for supplying the mines with beef."

Most likely, the first cattle in Siskiyou County were derived from the riding or packing stock brought in first by trappers, then by early settlers. Forage being plentiful and conditions good, it was not difficult to begin breeding. By April 1882, prices were higher than they'd ever been; stockmen received 6¢ a pound for beef on the hoof, or $35 to $40 for a good steer. In addition, with the advent of the railroad in 1887, production continued to soar and the towns of Montague and Gazelle became important shipping stations. The Siskiyou County Chamber of Commerce reported that 60,000 head of cattle moved through these two points annually, though many of those cattle were driven in from points east or west, from Scott Valley or Oregon.

Cattle raising along the Salmon or Klamath River, where deer were plentiful, was not a large industry, though a handful of ranches kept dairy cows for milk. At Sawyer's Bar, there were only a few owned by Abe Ahlgren. And, according to one old-timer, these "old cows" grazed on "used toilet paper" from the outhouses, so that the local kids didn't want to drink the milk.

There were just a few larger ranches along the rivers where market or beef cattle were raised. Some of the stock brands from this region included the LeDuc brand from Scott Bar; the Bratt, Jensen, Everill, Johnson, Hubbard, Lichens, Morgan, and David Collins brands from Oak Bar; the R. Rainey, Lowden Brothers, and Phillips brands from Seiad; and the James Rainey and S.M. Gosney brands from Hamburg. The Parker Ranch, however, in Plowman's Valley on the East Fork of Scott River, above Callahan's, was one of the largest cattle ranches established in Siskiyou County. Alexander Parker and his wife, Susanna, came to Scott Valley in 1854 and, in 1856, they bought land in Plowman's Valley. The AP cattle brand is one of the earliest brands of Siskiyou County.

Another early Scott Valley cattle ranch that is celebrating its 150th anniversary is the Smith Ranch, located on the Island Road, 2 miles north of Etna. George F. Smith, born in England in 1825, settled in Scott Valley in 1852, after purchasing a large parcel of land. He returned to Connecticut in 1858 and returned with his bride, Miss Cleopatra Fairbrother. From this marriage, six children were born. It is interesting to note that one of his daughters, Minnie E. Loos, became the mother of Anita Loos, renowned screenwriter whose fame included "Gentlemen Prefer Blondes" and other Hollywood productions.

REICHMAN'S STORE. The Etna "branch" of Reichman's store featured merchandise of every sort. (Courtesy Jenner Family Collection.)

An early Fort Jones rancher was Israel S. "Matt" Mathews, who, along with John Fairchild, drifted into Scott Valley in 1852. Mathews homesteaded 160 acres right in the middle of town; that is, where Fort Jones now sits. He named his ranch the Star Ranch, then married Ann Elizabeth Coffin, who had come into the valley with the Davidson family. Story has it that with each child he added another 160 acres, ending up with a sizeable operation. Mathews and his seven sons later opened up butcher shops, five in all. Meanwhile, John Fairchild went up McAdams Creek to Deadwood, then over to Yreka to settle.

One Etna pioneer was E.P. Jenner, who came to Scott Valley first in 1849 then left, only to return after gold was discovered. In 1864, in response to the growing need for a mill, he assumed management of the Union Flour Mill, owned in part by Fritz Holzhauser, who later deeded his portion and left for South America, only to settle in Sacramento. Located between the Smith Ranch and the Wagner Ranch, on the east side of what was called Hughes' Hill, this mill could produce 30,000 bushels of flour a day. Marie Holzhauser eventually sold the mill to Charles Jenner and joined her husband in Sacramento. E.P. Jenner's nephew Frank S. Jenner later followed him to California and Scott Valley where he

EARLY LOGGING. Perched on a springboard, a logger stands beside a giant redwood. (Courtesy Siskiyou County Museum.)

eventually bought the Jim Davidson ranch. The ranch is still owned and operated by descendants of Frank Jenner.

Other ranches to celebrate nearly 150 years of continued operation include the Glendenning Ranch and the Bryan Ranch on the eastern side of the valley (the Bryans descend from James Bryan, a soldier who served at Fort Jones, and the Hovendens); the Hammond Ranch, down Scott River; and the Hayden Ranch, with extensive acreage outside Etna and near Callahan. Several other old-time Scott Valley ranching and farm operations include those of the Denny, Hovenden, Young, Horn, Walker, Simas, Davidson, Dowling, and Costa families.

Logging also prospered in the aftermath of the Civil War. Along the Klamath, Scott, and Salmon Rivers, sawmills were established in dozens of places, too numerous to identify. Most were run by water power, some by steam, and later ones by gas-powered engines. Cut trees were moved down river to the sawmills or hauled out by high-wheeled wagons and teams. Oxen were also used for moving timber; according to Carol Pitts Maplesden in the *1996 Siskiyou Pioneer,* "They [the oxen] would never lunge with a load like many horses but naturally leaned into it until it moved . . . Such bulls had a very low market value and made good work animals." The Maplesden Sawmill was located at Hamburg, where Whit and Ben also did carpenter work. Ben Maplesden "built many of the huge water wheels used in the mining operations on Klamath River." They owned a second mill at Doggett Creek.

At Spencer Creek, Granville Naylor and John Hockenyose sawed lumber for settlers in both southern Oregon and northern California. At Klamathon, near present-day Hornbrook, was another mill. Logs were sent down a chute to the river below, then driven downstream. There were mills at Ditch Creek (Walsh and Parker), Ash Creek (Tom Clyburn), Barkhouse Creek (Lange Brothers), Beaver Creek (Jim Clyborn), and Horse Creek. There was the Swartz Mill at Hamburg and Walter Morgan's Mill in Hamburg Gulch. Mills at Happy Camp included Ralph Turk's and Shelton & Gordon. On Indian Creek was the Van Brunt Mining Company, the Howard Brothers, and the Andrew Horth's Mills. There were also mills at Cottage Grove, on Coon Creek, Buzzard Hill, Independence Creek (Bunker Hill Mine), Seiad, and Clear Creek. Many mills came later, including Charles Quigley's Mill, the Jensen Mill, and the mill at Roger Ranch operated by Dick and Charles Doggett.

Early sawmills on the Salmon River included the Lord-Ghent Sawmill in Nordheimer Creek; a mill at Crapo Creek, which, operated before 1860, was likely one of the earliest; the Bennett Company Mill at Forks of Salmon; the Orcutt Mill on Methodist Church; the Sightman's Mill at Yokumville; Brown's Mill at Petersburg, also one of the earliest; the Ahlgren's Mill on North Fork; the Bigelow Mill and the Yank Barrows Mill, both at Sawyer's Bar; and the John Hughes and Fergundez's Mills in Eddy's Gulch.

LOGGING WITH HIGH WHEELS. Logging grew in importance as methods of hauling the logs became more efficient. (Courtesy Betty Hall–Irene Jordan Nelson Collection.)

On the Scott River watershed, early mills were run by the Eastlick family, David Jones, Brockaw, and Manley, and later, Lafe Lewis, all in Quartz Valley. Manuel Periria and, later, the Miller Brothers, the Pinkerton family, Byrne and Wayne, Marshall Crawford, and Bill Evans ran mills in or near Fort Jones. Egli ran a mill on Kidder Creek, Dikon Lee ran a mill in Etna and Al Lee ran a mill on Yreka Mountain. Cramer's Mill was located on Moffett Creek.

At the southern end of Scott Valley, on French Creek, was the Sugar Creek Pine Company. Bernita Tickner, whose father worked as a sawyer at this mill, recalls that a Native American cemetery had been located nearby. Hjertager and Son had a band mill in Callahan, as did William Munson. There was the Schmitt Mill on Houston Creek between Callahan and Gazelle, and J.W. Kyle's Mill on Duzel Creek.

Needless to say, there were dozens of mills built all over Western Siskiyou County that survived for short periods of time. Many of them, hand-operated mills using whipsaws, had no names or have been forgotten. Still others opened up at the turn of the century or later, as logging became a major component of Siskiyou County's economic base. Pulled by oxen or mules were wagons with high wheels. Such work was dangerous and demanding. The earliest record load measured 14,958 board feet and was pulled by a team of 10 oxen.

Other businesses that sprang up in the county during this early post-war period likewise became successful. One such business in Rough and Ready and around Western Siskiyou County was the Kappler Brewery. Charles Kappler, born in Alsace, France in 1834, came to the United States in 1857. He settled briefly in Yreka, then returned to France to marry Florentine Kriner. In 1867, the couple returned to Yreka, then bought a brewery from P.A. Hartstrand on the east side of Scott Valley in 1868. He moved the operation to town in 1872. Although fire wiped out the original building, a second operation was built that greatly expanded the enterprise.

Kappler's Brewery reportedly netted $250,000 annually and became well known throughout northern California. It even won a blue ribbon at the World's Fair. The Kappler house, a three-story structure on Main Street, was torn down in the 1960s, but in the course of its existence, it served as the first Catholic church, as a school, and as a doctor's office. Kappler was also noted for building the first ice plant in Scott Valley and for providing the first electric lights to the people of Etna in 1898.

From the beginning, Etna prospered. School, first taught in the Etna Hotel owned by Wilkes and Brown, then moved to the mill on Main Street (now the site of the Etna Masonic Hall). The Rough and Ready School District was officially established in 1859 and the Etna district, called the Center School District, in 1865. This name was later changed to the Etna School District in 1873. Then, in 1874 by an act of legislature, Rough and Ready/Aetna Mill were merged, and the official name became Etna Mills. Later on, the "Mills" was dropped and the town came to be known as Etna. In 1892, Etna took on the distinction of having the first high school north of Red Bluff, California.

KAPPLER HOUSE, ETNA. The home of Charles Kappler, founder of the Etna Brewery, was built in 1895. (Courtesy Jenner Family Collection.)

Etna continued to remain an active trading post throughout the end of the nineteenth century for pack train companies and freight companies. Mule trains employed approximately 150 pack mules during the 1870s. According to the *1962 Siskiyou Pioneer*, some of the early, well-known freight and pack trains included those owned by Bill Bennett of the Forks of Salmon, the Eller Brothers (Elza and Aaron) of Etna, the Eldridges of Etna, the Herbie Finley train, the Isaacs train, and the Grant pack train. John and Harry Grant operated a hotel and store at Snowden, though they packed out of Etna.

Always of concern was the possibility of a hold-up. One occurred on Scott Mountain in 1870. Two highwaymen stopped the California & Oregon Stage, but Johnny Reynolds, the Wells Fargo & Company's messenger, happened to be inside the coach. When he saw what was happening, he shot and killed one of the bandits. The other managed to escape.

On October 10, 1894, a stage coach robbery took place, as reported in the *Yreka Journal*: "On Tuesday of last week, about 10:30 a.m, the Scott Valley stage, in charge of Dan Cawley, with six passengers on board, was stopped by a masked man pointing a well-oiled rusty revolver at the driver, near the foot of the Forest House mountain divide, on the Scott Valley side, half a mile north of Joe Wilson's place." After demanding only the treasure box, the bandit sent the stage on its way. He managed to get away with only $100 in coin.

FREIGHT WAGON TO SALMON. Getting ready to move out, this freight wagon is parked in front of the Welsey Saloon and Hadcock Hotel in Etna. Mike Balfrey stands on the sidewalk. (Courtesy Hayden Family Collection.)

Another Etna pack train was the Peters line. Originally begun by John Peters in 1894, he and another packer were killed coming from Sawyer's Bar on skis, after getting caught in a snow slide near Rocky Point. According to Lorraine Peters, the party carrying the mail came out an hour ahead, but when Peters and his partner did not arrive at Etna Mills, search parties were sent out. The two mens' bodies were found after tracks were discovered leading into the slide area, but not back out. The rescuers had to search the area using long poles. After John Peters's death, his wife remarried and the business became the Peters-Neilon train.

Other pack trains known throughout the area included Gus Meamber's pack train, the Denny Bar company train (out of Callahan), the H.D. McNeill train (out of Cecilville), and the A. Brizzard and Sons pack trains (out of Humboldt County). Brizzard and Sons often came in the fall of the year to haul freshly milled flour, grain, and creamery butter back to their stores at Somes Bar, Orleans, Weichpec, Martin's Ferry, and even Hoopa.

According to Bill Balfrey, a modern-day packer, mules in these early strings were so well trained they knew their place in the line-up. With saddles and packs set out in a long line, the mules would go and stand in front of their loads. Often, a blind was used to cover their eyes so that they would remain as calm as possible while being packed. Though today's pack mules rarely carry over 150 pounds, mules in the old days often packed loads of 300 pounds.

Fort Jones also prospered during the last decades of the nineteenth century. The Diggles brothers built the first store in town and, in 1861, they built the first brick structure in the valley. The brothers then parted company and Henry, in company with others, built the first steam flouring mills that serviced the entire valley and adjoining mining districts. Henry Diggles remained active in the Masons, Independent Order of Odd Fellows, and participated in all kinds of local charities and associations.

The first church established in Fort Jones was the Methodist Church. Built in 1873 on the flat below Dr. Cabiness's residence, near an old Native American burial ground, it was dedicated on June 24, 1874. The building cost $1,600. The Fort Jones Roman Catholic Church held its first services in a hall under the direction of Father Farley; construction of a church didn't begin until 1881 when Israel S. Mathews, one of Scott Valley's earliest pioneers, donated a piece of land. After that, the women of the church raised more than $1,500 in a matter of days.

In 1893, the Fort Jones Episcopal Church was erected on the corner of Main and Sterling Streets, site of the Sterling Hotel that was destroyed by fire. For a time, muslin hung in the empty windows because money had run out. John Kramer, who owned a livery stable on the site of the present Scott Valley Bank, donated $1,500 so that glass could be installed. Unfortunately, membership in the church declined soon after and the building was sold to the city. It was converted into the city hall, jail, library, and fire hall, until it was torn down for a new fire hall many years later.

ELLER PACK TRAIN. Each mule stands in front of "his" pack and saddle, c. 1915. (Courtesy McBroom Family Collection.)

The old school, which was for a time held under the Odd Fellows' Hall, became too cramped as student numbers increased. Trustees David Horn, E. Reichman, and H.J. Diggles solved the problem by renting the Hank Wright building (across the street from the Sterling Hotel) for the upper grades. But it wasn't long before principal and teacher George W. Oman was retired, so unpopular was he with students and parents. According to one story, retold by Harry H. Green, a student, Irish-born Mike Marlahan, received an unexpected "whack" across his shoulders from Mr. Oman's leather strap on his first day of school. When the boy asked his neighbor Harry Green, "Phat the divel did he sthrike me for," Harry had no reply.

Horseracing became a passion for many of the locals throughout Siskiyou County. Adam Baker Carlock's racehorse "Rattler" was a well-known racer in the early 1870s. Carlock, a Fort Jones pioneer and entrepreneur, owned a mercantile store in Fort Jones in 1860 and served as postmaster, but is most remembered for opening the first bank in Western Siskiyou County in 1867 (later bought by Scott Valley Bank).

Other early horse breeders included McVay and Evans of Scott Valley; the Edson Brothers of Shasta Valley; William Eckart of Yreka; Al Peacock of Yreka; the Ball Brothers of Butte Creek Valley (with a horse titled "Giraffe," the tallest horse known at over 18 hands); James Vance of Yreka; David Horn of Fort Jones; G. Cummings of Scott Valley; William McConnell of Yreka; Mrs. Sutherland; E. Flitner of Yreka; J.M. Chauncy of Fort Jones; J.M. Walbridge of Yreka; and F.M. Ranous of Little Shasta.

FORT JONES ELEMENTARY SCHOOL. This school picture was taken on December 20, 1892. Anna Mahan Beem was the teacher. (Courtesy Irene Nelson–Betty Hall Collection.)

In the next decades, the Wagners of Etna also boasted exceptional horses, as did Pete and Martin Larson, Burt Altafer, Bob Luttrell, and Bill Shelley.

Other favorite forms of entertainment included baseball, band concerts, and dances. Long a favorite pastime around Siskiyou County, baseball was especially supported by the locals. In 1875, Yreka beat Butteville 99 to 27. In 1892, Fort Jones beat Etna 65 to 16. The McAdams Creek baseball team of 1883 included players George Lincoln, William Davies, Frank Hegler, Ted Lincoln, Horace Mitchell, George Stage, John Hart, Tom Hegler, and Ed Mathewson.

One of the two most talked about events in Western Siskiyou County during the last decade was the great flood of February 8, 1890:

> Sunday came, and with it rain, which increased as the day advanced. Near nightfall, just as Moffett Creek threaded its way through the snow to join the torrent already rushing down the mountainside through Sterling Street [of Fort Jones], the rain increased in volume. It was a night of anxious watching . . . On Monday morning the water began to encroach upon the buildings which stood well back toward the stream; it came between the houses and the farther buildings. Near noon snow covered the water like giant fleeces of wool; the torrent rolled as if some pent-up reservoir had been loosed.

By Thursday, "barns, buildings and fences on the west side of town from Isaac Hamilton's to Chinatown were more or less damaged . . . The Ohio House bridge across the river, the slough bridge and the Goodale bridge are gone, and the new bridge at the mouth of Scott River is reported gone."

Another important event that occurred in Scott Valley was the big fire of March 16, 1896 in Etna. As reported in *The County Reporter*:

> The cry of fire was sounded at about 1:30 o'clock this morning. It aroused the slumbering people of the town, who, half awake and half clad, rushed from all directions on to Main Street to find that Mrs. Mani's hotel and saloon building was in flames and past all hope of being saved . . . As is well known, this end of the block was covered with wooden buildings from Emil Miller's brick store around to Odd Fellows Hall, and no hopes were entertained of saving any of them from the first, as the flames spread very rapidly from the Mani Hotel to James Bryan's variety store and the post office, then to Schmitt's hotel, and so on around to the building owned by David Jones and occupied by L.A. Moxley, where the flames stopped . . . All efforts, therefore, were directed to keeping the fire confined to the doomed district . . . A hard fight was made at the blacksmith shop of R. J. Wallace . . . On the porch in front of this building stood men throwing bucket after bucket of water over the front of the building and over themselves as it was passed up by willing hand.

WILLIE WAGNER. Known for breeding fine horses, Willie Wagner stands here with his prized horse Blondie. (Courtesy Hayden Family Collection.)

Life was not easy in the early days of Western Siskiyou County. Diseases—never uncommon in nineteenth-century America—flourished during the post-war period. Cholera was not uncommon in the mining camps. Diphtheria and other childhood diseases took the lives of many children; John K. Luttrell of Fort Jones lost his two eldest children within a few weeks of each other. Scarlet fever hit Fort Jones and Yreka during January and February 1869, and smallpox was discovered near Jacksonville, Oregon in February 1869. In response to the outbreak, Yreka immediately imposed a strict quarantine and promoted a vaccination program. As a result, while more than 40 people died in or around Jacksonville, only seven or eight (all in the Castro family) died in Hawkinsville, a few miles north of Yreka. Unfortunately, 600 smallpox victims died in San Francisco.

Fear arose again in 1880 when diphtheria reappeared, and again in 1883 in Fort Jones when more cases occurred. Henley (north of Yreka), then known as Cottonwood, suffered under the blows of 89 cases in February, March, and April of 1884.

It is not surprising that in the recorded history of Western Siskiyou County, much was written about local doctors. And there were many favorites. One such early doctor was Dr. Joel Newton, who began practice in 1862. A Civil War veteran, he became famous for his successful practice and reasonable fees (often taking none). Many stories have circulated about Dr. Newton's achievements; one involved a boy whose nose had been bitten off by a "vicious stallion." Dr. Newton successfully replaced the end of the nose, lauded still as "the first tissue graft ever performed in Siskiyou County." In another incident, Frank Hooper recalled how, as a boy, he suffered from an abscess in his cheek. Dr. Newton, seeing him on a street corner, "sharpened an old pocket knife on his boot and proceeded to open it and send me home without further dressing or attention to it," with "good results." Dr. Newton was also famous for his stable of fine horses and his faithful mule Juanita.

Dr. C.W. Nutting arrived in Etna in September 1878. A graduate of Atlanta Medical College, he was a "dashing, young 26-year old bachelor" when he first came. He married Jennie Parker, daughter of Alexander and Susannah Parker, in 1881. Jennie, who had eight brothers "learned to hold her own with menfolk." She was an adept rider. The two quickly became well loved and well known for their generosity, deep faith, and love of education. Along with their 7 children (4 others died in infancy), they took in 20 other students so that they could attend school. Even the local high school teachers resided with the Nutting family.

Dr. Nutting practiced medicine in Scott Valley and the surrounding areas for 39 years, never refusing to attend anyone, no matter the weather or distance. Serving as his assistant when surgery was required was William J. Balfrey, the second Etna druggist (James A. Diggles was the first). Balfrey, who also kept saddle horses and a buggy team on hand for such medical emergencies, would administer chloroform or ether, which came into use during this time. When Charles Nutting died, his books revealed that "at least $100,000 was owed him," a fortune in those days. Two more generations of Nutting doctors followed in Charles W. Nutting's footsteps.

Dr. William H. Haines was also a popular doctor. First entering practice with Dr. Nutting, he established his own practice in 1899. He married the daughter of Charles and Florentine Kappler, Eugenia Mary Kappler, who was a talented artist and musician. Dr. Haines practiced medicine in Etna for 51 years until he and Eugenia moved to San Francisco. There are many anecdotes about his travels. As retold in the *1962 Siskiyou Pioneer*, in one incident, Haines and Joseph Walker, who had accompanied him on his call, became stranded in a blizzard on Scott Mountain. In order to keep from freezing to death, "they started a fire with his raccoon coat which his mother had sent him from Illinois." In another incident, he "performed an appendectomy on a patient at a mine near Cecilville on a kitchen table, with limited surgical equipment and used thread for sutures. There was no way to move the man except by horseback down the snow-covered trails."

Dr. Edwin W. Bathurst, with his wife, Anne Mary Hutchins, and baby, came to Sawyer's Bar around 1877. Dr. Bathurst "rode mules, horses, and once a donkey to mines or homes in the Salmon Country, ministering to the needs of the people." After five years, the doctor moved his family to Etna and there set up his practice, a practice that lasted for 62 years. An avid gardener, he and his wife raised four children. Two boys died in infancy during the diphtheria epidemic at Sawyer's Bar.

Dr. Daniel Ream, who stood over 6 feet and was a comsumate horseman, was at times popular and then controversial. Coming to Siskiyou County with a band

FORT JONES PIONEERS. Pictured here in 1858 are, from left to right, Charles Hovenden, A.B. Carlock, Dr. Ream, and Dan Luttrell. (Courtesy Mike Bryan Family Collection.)

of cattle, Ream's first aspiration was to mine. He settled on Humbug Creek but, before long, entered actively into medical practice. He opened a drugstore at Deadwood in 1856. While living there, he entered politics and was elected Siskiyou County coroner in 1859. He moved to Yreka, the new county seat, where he also continued his practice. In 1861, Dr. Ream was elected sheriff; in 1867, he was elected tax collector. In 1877, he was elected state senator and served the counties of Modoc, Siskiyou, Shasta, and Trinity. Dr. Ream was married twice and had four children, two of whom died in childhood. An intelligent man, he pursued many hobbies or interests: farming, horses, mining, patent rights for a butter churn, newspapers, drugstores, politics, and lodge service, principally the Masons.

Because of his political aspirations, however, Dr. Ream was criticized frequently. This was especially true when, in 1870, he sold his home and property to the Board of Supervisors for a hospital "at a price considered, by many, excessive." At the same time, he was commended on his service as a state senator and as a physician; he would travel great lengths, even falling asleep in the saddle while snow fell around him. According to Chester Barton, in his memoir (see *Memories from the Land of Siskiyou*, edited by Davies and Frank), "he'd go anyplace, anytime, whether there were roads or whether it was on the other side of the Klamath. He had a team of horses and a buckboard and he even swam across the river to get places. In his latter days, he had a big white horse." For 50 years, Dr. Ream tended patients throughout the county. To many, he was one of the county's most prestigious pioneers. He died in 1906.

Dr. J.B. Robertson was a popular doctor in Yreka and the surrounding area. Unfortunately, after a fall from a horse while making a call along the Klamath River, he suffered internal injuries and died on August 15, 1878. He was 32 years old. Sadly enough, his 22-year-old wife died only a few months later while visiting her husband's family in Georgia. A 3-year-old daughter was left orphaned.

In many of the area's early towns and communities, however, there were no doctors. Lydia Head, writing in her memoirs, noted that in Sawyer's Bar "for years there was no doctor. Lard and turpentine was a panacea for many ills such as colds, pleurisy and pneumonia. Usually this medication was followed by large doses of castor oil. Then, as spring approached, we would take sulfur and molasses to thin the blood." Lydia Head lived to be 102 years old; she died in 1979.

PACK TRAIN IN SNOW. Packing in supplies to Salmon River continued during the winter months. (Courtesy Siskiyou County Museum.)

4. THE NEW CENTURY THROUGH WORLD WAR I

The new century ultimately brought significant changes to Western Siskiyou County. First of all, towns were becoming well established, though many of these communities would not survive beyond World War I. Schools were opening up even in the remotest portions of the region, though most were only one-room schoolhouses.

Women were taking a more active political and social role in the emerging businesses and government, and were accomplishing new things every day. The array of inventions and technology being introduced all over the nation hinted at changes of great impact, but apart for electric lights installed in Etna in 1898, for those citizens isolated in the rural mountain valleys of Western Siskiyou County, life in the early years of the twentieth century seemed pretty much the same as always.

As people settled into family life and town life, there was an increased amount of leisure time. Social life and sporting events blossomed. Almost every community boasted a concert band that played for parades, dances, and celebrations. Fort Jones, Happy Camp, Yreka, Etna, Sawyer's Bar, even Oro Fino—where nothing remains but the sink hole left by dredgers and mining operations—enjoyed its music. Tickets sold for "A Grand Benefit Ball, in the new music hall, September 2, 1898," only cost "one dollar for ticket and supper."

Dances were major events and marked every holiday and season, either in ballrooms, which had been built as part of most hotels or as separate halls, or in outside pavilions or homes. The Maplesden Hall in Etna, the Western Hotel and the Dance Hall in Fort Jones, and the halls in Greenview and Callahan were a few of the popular locations in Scott Valley for dances.

Speaking to Bernita Tickner, Mary Harris Hammer recalled that electricity came to Greenview in the early 1900s. "I can recall the first radio in Atwater Kent's . . . The radio was a big one and everyone turned out to put up a big antenna behind the hall."

Mary also recalled that "Bert Palmer drove a jitney stage [a Model-T Ford] which later became the school bus that took us kids to Etna High School . . . It had isinglass curtains and wooden seats."

Christmas was an especially happy time, with dances and a giant tree. "Mother made gifts for everyone," recalled Mary, "and for Earl Egli a pot of baked beans."

Oro Fino Band. From left to right are Frank Quigley, Bill Lewis, Willsie Whipple, Willard Eastlick, Jim Whipple, Frank Whipple, Lafe Eastlick, Grant Lewis, Ed Eastlick, and (?) Eastlick. (Courtesy Muzinich Family Collection.)

Chester H. Barton, in his memoir, related the following:

> Lots of times, when we went to dances [in the early 1900s], we used to put our clothes in a flour sack. We'd wear old clothes because we'd go to Scott Bar in the mud in the wintertime or dust in the summertime . . . When they had the big dances, they would have an orchestra come down from Etna—the Smith Brothers—or from Yreka. We always had a big banquet—a dance dinner. Two dollars and fifty cents a ticket usually paid for yourself and your girl . . . Sergeant Sambo would do the cooking.

And in his memoir of Scott Bar, Edward Leduc wrote, "Most of the dances consisted of the Waltz, Two Step, Schottische, Polka and Quadrills and would last until five or six in the morning, when they would pick up and start for home with the horse or horses and buggies."

Sports grew in popularity during the early years of the new century. Local teams gained fame and garnered support, especially the winning teams. In 1901, Etna had a "champeen" baseball team, featuring the following line-up: George Smith in right field; Ernest Messner in center field; George Buchner in left field; Matt Smith at first base; Fred Clute at second base; Patterson at third base; Roy Baker at short stop; Martin Messner as catcher and second base; and Wesley Messner, Harding, and Bicknel as subs.

The 1911 Etna baseball team, managed by Robert Willard, won a record 13 games in a row and earned the title "Wonder Team of Siskiyou"; their greatest joy was in beating Yreka on the Fourth of July for a purse of $175. Early basketball teams, both boys and girls, often traveled by stagecoach to compete against Yreka and by train to compete against Medford or Ashland. At home, Scott Valley fans filled Maplesden Hall. Tennis was introduced at Etna High School in 1916. Football was played when numbers were sufficient.

Fourth of July celebrations were important social events throughout the region. At Forks of Salmon, Bill Bennett opened his general store and "everything was for the people. That day was for the people." At Happy Camp, according to Bernice (Kenney) Sutcliffe Sedros (see *Memories from the Land of Siskiyou*), "We had dances maybe twice a month. On the Fourth of July weekend, we had three dances. During the day we'd have a ball game. We'd dance from eight or nine until daylight. It was just old clean fun." She added, "We'd walk to dances, dance all night, then walk home. From Clear Creek to Happy Camp. That was ten miles."

Leduc related, "Fourth of July celebrations started with a picnic lunch including lemonade, other soft drinks, ice cream (homemade), and watermelon. In the afternoon there would be a ballgame, foot races, egg races, once or twice there were horse races . . . About dusk there would be a few firecrackers and a few fireworks."

Parades were common, marked by floats, patriotic banners, and displays, in addition to bands and school children marching to music. As the century

ETNA WOMEN'S BASKETBALL TEAM, 1910. The team was photographed in front of the first Etna High School building. (Courtesy Hayden Family Collection.)

FOURTH OF JULY PARADE.
This women's suffrage group
parade passed through Sawyer's
Bar as part of the 1913 Fourth
of July parade. (Courtesy
Siskiyou County Museum and
Betty Young Collection.)

unfolded, a common parade entry included groups of suffragettes. There were also celebrations honoring the early pioneers and the newly established organizations, including the Masons, E Clampus Vitus, the International Order of Odd Fellows, and the Native Sons and Daughters of the Golden West. The Knights of Pythias, as well as the Grange, also emerged as important and vital organizations.

Both the Masons and International Order of Odd Fellows grew quickly in Western Siskiyou County. Sporadically, these two organizations—with links to the East—offered a great structure that brought order and brotherhood into the rough-and-tumble mining communities. The Evening Star Lodge, No. 186, was first organized on October 10, 1867. The first Master was Abisha Swain and he directed the construction of the Masonic Hall in 1867. In 1872, members voted to procure a charter. Abisha Swain was named "worthy patron"; Emily C. Swain was voted "worthy matron"; Mrs. Ann Diggles, was elected secretary. The organization has continued to meet in the same location for more than 130 years.

The International Order of Odd Fellows (IOOF) first met at the Temperance Hall in "the Beehive" in Etna, on March 30, 1870. Their first building also housed the Etna school, but when student numbers increased, a new brick building was built on a lot bought from Jacob Messner in 1881.

In 1911, the Native Sons of the Golden West began construction on a new building in Fort Jones. As reported in the September 6 issue of *Farmer and Miner,* young "Martin C. Beem, Jr., laid the first brick of the fine projected hall of the Native Sons of the Golden West."

E Clampus Vitus (ECV) was also a fraternal organization that grew up with the gold rush. Loosely structured, it had few rules or regulations; in fact, it poked fun at the serious lodges and their rituals. In ECV, "every member holds an office of equal indignity," and its stated purpose was "to care for the widows [of miners, originally] and orphans, but especially the widows." Today, the Humbug Chapter of ECV, centered in Fort Jones, is still a carefree organization, but it does contribute to local historical preservation, charities, and causes.

The Order of the Native Daughters of the Golden West (NDGW), according to Bernita Tickner, was established as a "fraternal and patriotic organization," whose primary goal was to support and broaden the understanding and appreciation of California's roots. NDGW, Eschschotzia Parlor No. 112, organized in July 1899, continues to do so by providing landmarks and maintaining historical records. It also maintains the Etna Museum, a newly remodeled facility, as well as provides scholarships to graduating high school students. Through its history, the group has taken a strong role in the community. In 1899, the group's first two officers were Mrs. Rosalia Crandall and Miss (Anna) Grace Johnson.

Farming underwent important changes in the new century. By the end of the first decade, there were a number of threshing machines in Scott Valley. Many of these early machines were called binders. They cut grain and gathered the grain into bundles that were hand-tied, then stacked into shocks. From there, they were picked up by hand and put on a wagon, then taken to a stationary threshing machine that was driven by steam engine. Next came horse-drawn threshing machines (e.g., the Harris machine). Power for harvesting was generated by the large wheels that carried the threshing machine and by the pull of the horses as they drew the machine forward; it was then transferred to the enclosed cylinder and moving parts. It wasn't long until harvesters were converted to gas-engine power, but they were still horse drawn. Improvements on even these machines continued until tractors were brought in.

Hay balers and loaders were also introduced. Most early balers were considered stationary, but were moved from hay shock to hay shock by horse teams. Hand-fed, these machines were labor intensive. Another early, unique baler was a fully stationary, horse-powered machine

As the horse that was harnessed to a draw bar walked in a circle, it generated reciprocating power to a plunger that compressed the hay inside the bale chamber. With every rotation, the horse had to jump the connecting rod (running from crank to plunger head). One of these unusual balers can be seen at the Trinity Museum in Trinity Center.

Attached to a wagon in the field and pulled by a team of oversized horses, the loader picked up hay from windrows, then moved it up the conveyor, and over the high rear of the loader. Two men were responsible for distributing the load as it came up the conveyor. The horses had to be gentle and steady so that the men didn't lose their balance as they worked to keep up with the moving hay. It was exhausting work.

Ernest Hayden, who "drove a newfangled hay loader" at Parker's Ranch in Plowman's Valley, recorded the following:

> On steep ground the wagon was loaded heavier on one side so it wouldn't tip over when it was turned at right angles to the slope. Then going downhill, the other side was loaded to balance it. When loaded, the driver would take off for the barn or stack to be unloaded by a Jackson Fork, the motive power of which was provided by a "derrick horse" that was usually driven by a youngster paid a dollar a day.

In 1918, Frank Horn and the Hayes brothers were among the progressive Scott Valley farmers who purchased Tracklayer tractors. According to the March 8 *Western Sentinel*, results were good: "The fact that these machines are delivering more goods than the makers claimed for them is a very pleasing feature of the transaction."

Hay and grain prices fluctuated greatly and were dependent on weather conditions. As reported in one newspaper of the day, though the 1910 hay and grain harvest had been damaged by early rains, the 1911 yield was good. In fact, it was so good, reported the *Farmer and Miner*, that "[Scott Valley] farmers are buying automobiles and paying 'spot cash' for them!"

SUMMER RAKING. This horse-powered buck rake was in use in the early twentieth century. (Courtesy Liz Dillman-Bowen Collection.)

Alfalfa seed took a jump in price during World War I, which was a boon to farmers like the Pitts family in Noyes Valley. Farmers were also being encouraged to raise more hogs since they were easy to grow, quick to multiply, and easily cured for safe handling. According to one commentator of the time, "The American hog became an exalted animal, commanding for the moment a rather more intent regard than the lion or the eagle; the hog populations was almost as much a concern to the government as manpower." Sugar, flour, and wheat products were also highly sought-after items needed for soldiers overseas, thus restrictions were placed on the purchase of those items at home. Individuals were permitted to buy 2 pounds of sugar at one purchase within cities and towns, up to 5 pounds in rural areas. Larger quantities were sold only to boarding houses, camps, mines, and remote ranches. A card-ration system was not introduced, but, according to one news article, "Hoarding would not be tolerated."

Demand for horses increased as the United States moved into war, as well. This helped the farmers and ranchers in Siskiyou County who raised them. The army, which had been buying up local horses since the days of the Modoc War of 1871, purchased 1,200 cavalry horses from the county during the Spanish-American War. In 1875, the Presidio in San Francisco bought replacement mounts for horses that had died of a contagious disease. In addition, according to the September 13, 1914 *San Francisco Examiner*, the English selected choice mounts for use during the Boer War; the Germans bought horses from the county during the Boxer Rebellion in China; and even the Russians bought up horses for use during the Russo-Japanese War. During World War I, horses were needed to pull cannon and for use in the cavalry. The army began supplying stud horses to several ranchers to use in reproduction, and it also subsidized or rewarded those who rounded up stray and wild horses.

Of course, horses or steam were major sources of power in Western Siskiyou County during the first part of the twentieth century, but it wasn't long before the automobile fascinated many. Only a handful of wealthier individuals could afford the new contraption, but it was heralded as a great improvement over horse and buggy, if only because "it would surely save lives." Today, we find the idea of automobiles being accident-free difficult to understand, but in those early days, runaways and horse-related accidents were frequent and serious, so these new, steady, and sturdy rigs must have appeared indestructible.

The quality of roads remained a persistent issue around the county, especially downriver where the winding, narrow gorge of the Klamath River made travel slow or nonexistent. In many people's eyes, this lack of connection made continued economic development difficult to initiate. As late as 1888, nothing more than wagon roads existed. Narrow and rough, they were just wide enough for freight wagons headed one way. It wasn't until 1891 that a road over Salmon Mountain was finally built.

As Brian Helsaple writes, those who lived in Seiad on the Klamath River had to negotiate the following:

WORLD WAR I HORSES. An important commodity in the war, horses were bred or trained for use overseas. Charlie Wicks was photographed with two horses that were later used to pull cannon in France. (Courtesy Betty Hall–Irene Nelson Collection.)

the miserable, rut filled, dusty-in-summer-muddy-and-slippery-in-winter, blocked by slides and fallen trees, #★!!@! road that was better walked than ridden. . . . One of the first to travel the area on something other than horseback or wagon was Cap [Lowden]'s brother, Thomas. He was not a good driver of this device [the automobile] but since there were few other vehicles or traffic on the trail, skill was not of much concern . . . The most important ability was to remember where the brake was.

A road was finally finished over Evans Mountain from Grider's Ferry at Seiad to the Evans Ranch on China Creek in 1891, but most roads were only improved little by little. Construction on the road from Orleans to Somes Bar was begun in 1917, the year the United States entered World War I. A concrete bridge over Moffett-McAdams Creek, near Fort Jones, on the road leading to Indian Creek and down Scott River, was begun in 1918. And, according to the December 19, 1919 *Siskiyou Standard*, Supervisor Barnum of the Fifth District sent out for bid the road from Cecilville to Petersburg, on the South Fork of Salmon.

The increasing need for improved or new bridges was a concern to the people along the rivers, who had to travel great distances. Ferries existed in many

BUS TO SAWYER'S BAR. Over rough and narrow roads, this early bus made its way over Salmon Mountain from Etna to Sawyer's Bar. Note the heads of the four young women sticking out of the bus "windows." (Courtesy Betty Young Collection.)

locations and most were free, but subject to water levels or weather. There was a good ferry at Seiad, called Grider's Ferry, which was used until 1909 when the river bridge was built. There were also ferries at Evans Ranch, called the Gordon Ferry, and in Happy Camp. Without these ferries, however, people were forced to ford the river. On the Klamath, fording the river was a dangerous task much of the year, as evidenced by the following harrowing event reported in the March 26, 1920 *Siskiyou Standard*:

> The body of James P. Wiuf, who was drowned while attempting to ford the Klamath river near Cottage Grove on horseback, February 26th last, was found early this week . . . On receiving word that her husband's body had been recovered, Mrs. Wiuf at once left Fort Jones to be present at the interment. To do this she was compelled to go from here to Happy Camp by auto, and then ride horseback twenty-seven miles to Aubrey's.

Locals knew that having real bridges might revitalize the smaller communities in Western Siskiyou County that were beginning to shrink as mining opportunities diminished. As Brian Helsaple wrote, regarding the bridge-building project in Seiad, "With the bridge coming [to be completed in 1909], the chance for a real town to develop in Seiad Valley began to inspire all sorts of possibilities."

Even in 1918, the accepted Klamath River road still ended in Happy Camp, but government engineer C.C. Morris was ordered to begin the survey of the proposed 60-mile highway between Happy Camp and Somes Bar. Nothing much more than a trail led to Orleans, but in the summer of 1919, work began on a new road. Crews worked upriver and down, and the Willits and Burr Company was given the contract to build the road from Crawford Creek to Blue Nose Bridge. Tom Bigelow was the road construction superintendent. By 1922, the Blue Nose Bridge was finished and the road—little more than a one-way lane—was open to Orleans. It became part of the state highway system in 1926 and is now Highway 96.

Unfortunately, many Scott Valley residents waited earnestly for the coming of the railroad. Articles were written about when the railroad would cross the valley on the way to the coast. Farmers and entrepreneurs looked to the railway as the answer to a much-needed boost to the economy. Even in 1919, hopes were still high, as evidenced by the December 19 *Siskiyou Standard*'s declaration: "The railroad is to be continued through the valley to the Pacific coast which will give us the world's market by water." But it never happened. Still today the railroad passes north and south through Yreka.

COVERED BRIDGE AT SOMES. *Before bridges like this one over the Salmon River were built, early settlers had to ford the rivers. The last two bridges were replaced in 1964. (Courtesy Betty Young Collection.)*

Economically, mining remained the dominant force during the first decade of the new century. Small strikes were still being reported in the local newspaper; however, many of those miners who had worked independently or in small groups were finding it difficult to finance their operations, thus money-backed companies were stepping in to take over. For instance, in September 1911, as reported in the Fort Jones's *Farmer and Miner*, the Golden Eagle and New York mines on Indian Creek were sold to Eastern "capitalists." Both of these mines had been good producers and plans were established to keep the newly refurbished mines running continuously. As noted in the article, "The opening of these mines means the return of prosperity to the old historic town of Hooperville, where in early days, a teeming mass of humanity sought fame and fortune, both of which abounded in plenty."

One such large operation was the Siskiyou Mines Company on the Klamath River. Having purchased over 1,000 acres between Thompson Creek and Happy Camp, the company owned possibly "the largest area of virgin ground in Northern California." In order to mine it, the company had to take water from Thompson Creek, and a flume, capable of carrying more than 300 inches of water of sufficient pressure, had to be built.

The company also set up a sawmill on Thompson Creek where 12,000 feet of lumber was cut each day. The lumber was needed for ditch or mine repairs and to build new flumes. Though the Siskiyou Mines Company worked these mines until 1917, after 1919, little mining was accomplished here.

Dredgers were introduced a little before the turn of the century and were run on rivers and creeks around Western Siskiyou County. These larger operations provided new job opportunities. The Distelhorst Dredge operated on the Klamath River, below Oak Bar, around 1898. One of the first dredgers was located at Callahan soon after electric power was brought into Scott Valley, in 1903. The Wade Dredger was built near Callahan in 1907 and all machinery had to be hauled over Yreka Mountain. Contracted by Gus Reichman, a 20-horse team was needed to move the 50-ton "spud" over the mountain. After scaling the mountain, 18 horses were required on level ground. Others who assisted in its hauling included Sam Parker and Fred Harbaugh. The first dragline to be used on the Klamath River was used by McConnell Bar Mining in 1905. In 1915, the Klamath Dredging Company began operations 2 miles above Oak Bar.

The Yuba Dredger Company moved into Scott Valley. This dredge, built at the mouth of Sugar Creek, was much larger than ones built earlier. It plowed up to within 1 mile of Callahan's Ranch until the hills narrowed and the boat could go no further. Turning downstream, it pushed through Scott River down to the Wolford Ranch. The Wolfords would not sell out, so the dredge moved upstream again. In all, it traveled downstream a little more than 4 miles over 15 years.

In 1911, the Alta Burt Gold Dredging Company moved a bucket line dredge from below Callahan to Trinity Center, a 34-mile trip over narrow, crooked roads and precarious bridges. Ernest Hayden, who was just a boy at the time, wrote the following:

I remember seeing one of these heavy loads being pulled across the old steel bridge just below Callahan by at least 32 horses or mules . . . It is a marvel to me how the animals were trained to obey the vocal command of the drivers, to act in unison to the degrees necessary to start, stop, and turn these heavy loads as was required to successfully haul them around the sharp turns and negotiate the many steep grades . . . As I remember it, and existing pictures will bear me out, the string of draft animals stretched out about 300 feet . . . This, and the moving of the Quartz Mill to Black Bear Mine with no road at all by Deacon Lee will stand as a memento to the resourcefulness of the pioneers of this era.

Another kind of mining also opened up in Western Siskiyou County, though only for a limited time. In 1914, the U.S. Geological Survey released a report on chromic iron production; in that year, there was a reported production of 591 long tons, valued at $8,715. At the same time, the Fort Jones's *Farmer and Miner* of August 6, 1915 announced the sale of four chromite mines near Dunsmuir, in southern Siskiyou County, to Clarence M. Oddie of San Francisco for $56,000.

Chromite, a black or bluish-black rock found in serpentine, is a metal used in the manufacture of steel, especially in the production of gun barrels, armored

YUBA DREDGE. Built at the mouth of Sugar Creek near Callahan, the Yuba Dredge was larger than earlier dredgers. Tailings from the dredging operations still line the river and creek banks up and down Scott Valley. (Courtesy Betty Young Collection.)

plate, and stainless steel. With demand for steel increasing with the onset of World War I, these new deposits of chrome were important to European countries for building tanks. Moreover, when the United States entered the war in 1917, its demand for steel multiplied as well. Immediately, the federal government sent out a plea for conservation of resources, as well as appropriated money for the assessment and mining of chrome ore. As one conservation measure, the 8,000 tons of steel used in the production of women's corsets was stopped. In its place, manufacturers produced masks and belts for the Army Medical Corps. Radiator manufacturers made guns, piano companies produced airplane wings, and automobile factories built airplane engines.

As a result of the increased demand for steel, the rush was on to find deposits. The Seiad Creek Mine, estimated at 265,700 tons in 1913, only produced 789 tons during World War I. Other chromite mines in upper Seiad Creek included the Emma Bell, the Anniversary, and Black Eagle. According to Ernest Hayden in *Along our History's Trail*, one chromite mine, belonging to Alonzo Bingham, "yielded 335 tons, 35 tons of which were lying on the surface as float." Other mines opened up around the county as well, with finds ranging from 10 to 550 tons, but most were relatively small. Unfortunately, because of limited access to the deposits and because the war ended in 1918, the demand for chrome, which had generated such enthusiasm, disappeared almost overnight. Not until World War II would there be a second rush to mine chrome in Western Siskiyou County.

The U.S. Forest Reserves (changed later to the U.S. Forest Service, or USFS) was established in 1905 and quickly became an element in the economic and

HAULING THE "SPUD." *A 20-horse team packs the 50-ton Spud to the Wade Dredge on the Scott River near Callahan. (Courtesy Mike Bryan Family Collection.)*

A. Brizard Store. Located at Somes Bar, this was one of several Brizard stores along the Klamath and Salmon Rivers. (Courtesy Siskiyou County Museum.)

political life of Western Siskiyou County. The first ranger in Scott Bar was Mr. Harvey. In 1906, a station was established up Indian Creek about 5 miles, then moved to Happy Camp in 1918. Morris Gordon was the first district ranger there, but by 1920, there were four guards, a trail crew, a ranger, and a dispatcher. Frank Harley, whose name is mentioned in numerous Salmon River memoirs, was one of the early rangers in the Salmon area; he traveled the road between Somes and Forks of Salmon by horseback.

After the USFS came in, telephones went in. Each house along the Salmon River and at Happy Camp had a phone furnished by the service. The new rangers assisted in installing the crank-type phones and telephone lines. Walt McCrary of Oro Fino hauled phone poles on wagons to Happy Camp. Interestingly, these wagons could be steered from either end to maneuver down the winding river roads. Returning to Sawyer's Bar after the war, Jim McNeill assisted in installing the telephone line from Finley Camp to the Keys Abbot Cabin.

The USFS in the early days helped keep the trails and roads open, cut trees where necessary, and established lookouts. USFS workers also broke stock to ride because the only way to haul supplies in and out of the fires was with animals, and the only way to navigate the rugged trails or terrain between locations was by horseback. It is interesting to note that in those first days of fire fighting, local people most often put out the fires before the USFS arrived. They submitted their time and would be reimbursed. Many locals, as mining became less profitable, took jobs with the USFS.

101

One such individual was William H. Hotelling. As related by his son Wes Hotelling, in *Memories from the Land of Siskiyou*, William Hotelling had been a miner all his life, mostly working as a laborer in larger mines. Living near Orleans, he left his family early every morning (4 or 5 a.m., even in winter) and crossed the Klamath River in a Native American canoe, which was often treacherous work. In 1906, however, he took a job with the USFS. First, he served as a guard, then as an assistant ranger. In his job, he helped maintain stock trails, which were used as fire trails, helped homesteaders clear their land or process their papers, and assisted in the clearing and surveying of land.

"He had to have a staff compass and chain—no tapes in those days!" Sometimes it was hard to establish section corners because of terrain and other difficulties, so it wasn't uncommon for a surveyor to "throw his hat in the air and where it came down this would be the corner." These newly surveyed parcels became homesteads for many old-time miners who were leaving their claims. William Hotelling left the USFS in 1911 when he took a job as general manager of Brizard (or Brizzard) Store at Somes Bar. He also became postmaster and justice of the peace. Wilbur Huestis replaced Hotelling as the forest ranger. Other rangers included Bob Finley, Christy Quigley, Bill Rider, Elam Orcutt at Yocumville, and Bill Gott.

THE LOOKOUT. *Hallie Daggett, the first woman lookout for the U.S. Forest Service, watches for fires. (Courtesy McBroom Family Collection.)*

Another job the USFS took on around 1910 was the collection of yellow pine seed for reforestation. As noted in one newspaper article, "It is expected that a large number of helpers will be employed in the gathering of the cones and in their subsequent treatment, in order to get the required amount of seed."

In 1920, 15-year-old Ernest Hayden of Callahan spent a summer as a fire lookout for the USFS. His job was to stay up on Mount Bolivar, located in the Scott River District of the Shasta National Forest, for the five- to six-month fire season. According to Hayden, "After my summer perched on this 8,400 foot mountain peak practically shaking hands with 30 million volts more or less of jagged chain lightning, I lost most of my fear of it at lower elevations."

One of the most notable individuals to reside in Western Siskiyou County and to serve in the USFS during the early portion of the century was a woman, Miss Hallie Morse Daggett. The daughter of John Daggett—miner, entrepreneur, retired superintendent of the U.S. Mint in San Francisco, and ex-lieutenant governor of California—Hallie was born and reared in the mountains surrounding Black Bear Mine. Hallie and her sister Leslie were competent outdoorswomen and most at home in the rugged terrain of the Klamath Mountains, even though both had been schooled at female seminaries in San Francisco and Alameda.

In 1913, to the chagrin of many, 30-year-old Hallie Daggett applied to the USFS for the position of fire lookout. Ranger McCarthy, after reviewing the qualifications of the three applicants (one was a drunk, the second had poor eyesight) chose Hallie. In recommending her, he wrote, "[she] is a wide-awake woman . . . who knows every trail on the Salmon River watershed, and is thoroughly familiar with every foot of the district. She is a perfect lady, in every respect, and her qualifications for the position are vouched for by all who know of her aspirations."

W.B. Rider, supervisor at the Klamath National Forest Office in Yreka, quickly approved the appointment in spite of the fact that Hallie would become the first woman fire lookout in the nation. Officially hired on May 26, 1913, she quickly drew recognition for her achievements. Hallie had always dreamed of living in a log cabin; her lookout, known as Eddy's Gulch Lookout Station, District Number 4, sat atop Klamath Peak. She noted in one of her many interviews, "[Around me] lay a seeming wilderness of ridges and gulches and pine—cedar, and fir-lined canyons."

Her cabin was a 12-foot by 14-foot structure, adorned only with an American flag that she faithfully raised each day. Hallie, who took her job seriously, knew that she was competing with every other lookout—all men—spread out across the Klamath Mountains. Commendations were given only to those who were vigilant and she was determined not to fail. In 1912, national forest fires had killed 75 people and devastated $25 million worth of timber. Hallie's primary job was to scan the forest in every direction for smoke; even at night, she scanned for signs of fire. At first, she used a telescope, but later she used binoculars. In the mornings and evenings she walked to the edges of the ridges to scan more carefully those

HALLIE DAGGETT. With her dog, Hallie spent 13 summers as a fire lookout for the U.S. Forest Service. (Courtesy Siskiyou County Museum.)

areas not easily seen from her lookout. Hallie was given only two days off a month and most often she returned to visit her family in Sawyer's Bar. But her sister Leslie was a frequent visitor, bringing up her mail and supplies every week. Other visitors came as well.

Indeed, Hallie was a keen observer. In her first season, she reported the most fires. Connected to the outside world by telephone, she recognized its importance when, during an electrical storm, it suddenly went dead. But little seemed to intimidate Hallie, who was at home on horseback or alone in the woods hunting, trapping, or fishing. Only when a panther began to stalk her did she begin strapping a pistol to her side.

Newspapers across the nation wrote about Hallie Daggett, with headlines like "Lonely Forest Post Guarded by Woman," or "Withal, First Woman Fire Warden is Very Feminine and Also Quite Efficient." In one *Sacramento Bee* article, dated July 12, 1913, District Ranger M.H. McCarthy declared "no man ever performed the duties more conscientiously or effectively."

By 1918, with the outbreak of war and a shortage of man-power, Hallie was no longer the sole woman on lookout. Two others were appointed that year and, by 1919, there were more women serving at fire lookouts than men. Hallie

Daggett died on October 19, 1964 and was buried in Etna next to her sister Leslie Daggett Hyde. It wasn't until 1988, however, that official tribute was given to Hallie's unmarked grave. The Eschschotzia Parlor No. 112, NDGW placed a plaque at the site.

Another outstanding woman in the early part of the new century who served Siskiyou County in an official capacity was Effie Persons. She was the first woman to fill the office of superintendent of schools, a position she held from 1898 until 1902, and then again from 1906 until 1910.

Grace A. Johnson (Balfrey), a graduate of Stanford University, also went on to become superintendent of schools. She was the daughter of Alexander Johnson, a Scott Valley pioneer who donated land to Etna High School, the Catholic Church, and for a city park. According to Bill Balfrey, grandson of Grace Johnson and Etna historian, "When Alexander died, Grace took two bars of gold, had it minted into coin, and left to attend school at Stanford." Grace later married William J. Balfrey of Etna, who had been the bell boy for the Smith Pack Train as a young boy.

Ruth Markon, born in Sawyer's Bar in 1898, went on to become one of Siskiyou's first female justices of the peace. She served the Salmon River district for more than 15 years.

BURCELL LOGGING. As the logging industry grew, small timber companies opened up hundreds of sawmills around the country. Hauling lumber became an important enterprise. (Courtesy Betty Hall–Jim Falkawski Collection.)

As mining waned, finding employment was becoming harder and harder for residents of Western Siskiyou County. Beginning in about 1906, many men chose to leave the area to log timber in adjoining counties. Because the logging industry was just beginning to boom, it attracted the young, ambitious, and restless. As a result, some of Siskiyou's young men never returned.

Coupled with that was the entry of the United States into World War I in January of 1918 and the passage of the Selective Service Act, also called the draft, in May of 1918. Dozens of Siskiyou's finest were drawn away. Promising adventure and glory, the war also provided an opportunity for work. Locals supported the war effort through contributions to the Red Cross, as well as through voluntary restrictions on food and fuel. Similar to the Sanitation Committees' support during the Civil War, local members of the Red Cross collected muslin and flannel bandages to be shipped for use in battlefront and state-side hospitals. Dances and other events were held as fundraisers.

Frank Harley, the district ranger at Orleans, recruited 11 young men from the Somes Bar area. Wes Hotelling was one of those who joined up. The boys left home in July 1917 and were inducted into the army at Fort McDowell on Angel Island. Herbert "Pat" Finley Jr. of Etna was one of the first to volunteer for service.

LYLE RITZ. Dressed in a World War I uniform, Lyle horses around. (Courtesy Betty Young Collection.)

PERRY HARRIS. As a young soldier in World War I, Harris died in France. The Scott Valley Chapter of the American Legion honored him by adopting his name for their chapter. He was photographed c. 1917. (Courtesy Kate Berthelson Collection.)

Henry Martin, the son of Tom and Kate (Duzel) Martin from Hamburg, was one of a number of Native Americans drafted into the army in 1917. According to Henry "Hank" Mostovoy (*Memories from the Land of Siskiyou*), Henry Martin's step-son, these boys

> gathered to catch the train for San Francisco but had to stay overnight in Yreka. Indians were not allowed to drink [as passed in 1915, called "The Squaw Man Act"]. However, this group felt if they were good enough to get killed they were good enough to drink. So they proceeded to throw a bartender out, closed and locked the door and got good and drunk.

After the sheriff was called in and matters brought under control, "the next morning, after cleaning up the bar, [they] caught the train. They never paid for the drinks believing payment to them was long overdue for living in their country."

George Martin, another Native American in his 20s, was also drafted into the army and sent to France and Germany. Later, he told how surprised he had been when he discovered he was able to go into the same places white soldiers went—even stores or restaurants. When the war was over, George moved to San Francisco.

Bill Smith, from Salmon River, also served in the army during World War I. Born at the Forks of Salmon Hotel, he was the grandson of W.P. Bennett, an early pioneer. Together with their father George Smith, Bill and his brother Ralph entered the freight and packing business before the war, then returned to it after the war in 1919.

Burrill Pitts of Plowman's Valley died from pneumonia while in France, and Charles Leo Wayne of Fort Jones died while serving on the *Tuscania*, the first United States troop ship torpedoed by a German submarine off the coast of Ireland. Private Perry LaForest Harris of Greenview also died in France. In his honor, the local American Legion adopted his name as its individual chapter name. Perry was the son of Charlie Harris, who owned a store in Greenview and served as postmaster. Perry's grandfather was John Cash Dyer, a miner in Oro Fino. Edward C. Delray from Fort Jones died on July 18, 1918 in France, and Clifford C. Hegler, brother of Mrs. Clyde O. Smith of Fort Jones, was severely wounded. Harold Arbuckle of Callahan, nephew of Mr. and Mrs. J.W. Facey of Etna, served as an aviator; he was later severely injured in a plane crash and lost sight in both eyes. Joe Starr was rejected for service for medical reasons.

The 20th Engineers (Forest) Regiment sought to recruit additional men from this area. Not of draft age, but between ages 18 and 40, these men were lumberjacks, sawmill workers, and men "experienced in building and operating logging railroads." This regiment joined the First Forest Regiment already in Europe, in cutting and transporting timber, lumber, and other forest products as needed in the war. Douglas Ames was one of those who enlisted in the 20th Engineers.

Many others served in World War I from Western Siskiyou County. From Sawyer's Bar, Almond Skillen and John E. Ahlgren enlisted. Allison Courts, who married Miss Mattie L. Evans of Fort Jones, served in the Field Artillery of the U.S. Army. Some other enlistees were Clifton Walker, Aviation Corps; Carl B. Smith, Electrical Engineering Corps; Jim McNeill, who also served during World War II; Bill Lee; William Jordan; Clifford Holmes; Joseph Gorman; Tom Glendenning; Frank Branson and Bernard E. Walker, both stationed at Camp Lewis; Frank "Bum" Ritz; Ted Spencer; John Golden; Charles Green; Silas Royal Pitts, in the Merchant Marines; and Doc Robinson. Some of those lost in the war included Ed Del Ray, Maud Evans, George Mathews, Leonard Schull, William Sheffield, Hallett Smith, Joe Silva, Frank J. Terra, and Charles Leo Wayne.

One event that scarred the local community involved the Joseph Dangel family of Quartz Valley. In 1890, 8-year-old Arthur Dangel, out collecting flowers and "oak puff balls" was brutally and fatally mauled by a mother lion and her cub. When Joseph Dangel found his son, who had been missing for more than two hours, he was dead, having been dragged off and partially eaten by the cats. A mother guarding her cub would have taken the boy for a threat. A hungry lioness looking for food would have thought him an easy target.

Neighbors rushed in and a hunt was on. A dead calf, laced with cyanide, was set out as bait and it didn't take the lions long to find it. Charlie Wicks was one of the men who came to assist in the hunt and Dangel knew he could trust the Shasta trapper to find the big cat. Charlie did indeed track the large lioness and her cub, and the event created a friendship between the families that has lasted generations. Others who assisted Charlie in the kill included Charles Howard and Al Kingsley.

The Dangel family was again hit with tragedy in 1911 when Arthur's older brother Albert drowned. He was 29 years old. Today's descendants of the Dangel family still reside in Scott Valley and include members of the Hayden and Denny families of Callahan. Albert was buried beside his younger brother.

As the second decade of the new century neared its end, Western Siskiyou County got its taste of a new era with the landing of an "Air Ship" on October 11, 1919. Everyone was invited to come and see the spectacular DeHaviland biplane, which arrived at 1 p.m. in the Reynolds' field outside Fort Jones (near the present junction of Eastside Road and Highway 3). According to Irene Nelson, who wrote about the event, adults and children thronged to inspect the plane. Later, she notes an airfield was built on "Pinky" Bill Mathews's ranch, called the Star Ranch, when flying became more common. Wing-walking became a great attraction and one Etna resident, "Perky" Knockstedt, as well as Carl Johnson of Yreka, thrilled audiences with daring stunts.

FIRST PLANE IN SCOTT VALLEY. *After landing on October 11, 1919 in Jas. Reynold's field near Fort Jones, F.P. McCarthy was photographed holding Francis Grider McCarthy (in little white cap). (Courtesy Betty Hall–Irene Nelson Collection.)*

5. The Depression and World War II

First passed in January 1919, the 18th Amendment, which ushered in Prohibition, had an immediate and incredible impact on the citizens of Western Siskiyou County. For most people, it was even more relevant than what was happening on the national or international level. First of all, liquor was a part of nearly every miner, farmer, or logger's diet. It was part of the culture of the day. Secondly, it adversely affected many small family businesses. The first to go included the Yreka and Etna Breweries, and the multitude of saloons or bars in the area. The Etna Brewery would not reopen until the 1980s when Andrew Hurlimann, the stepson of one of Kappler's descendants, purchased the property and reissued the original Etna Brewery label. Etna Brewery has become a well-respected microbrewery, now owned by David Krell.

Rather than intimidating local home distillers, however, the 18th Amendment set into motion a whole new industry. According to Thomas "Tom" Bigelow, in his memoir *Memories from the Land of Siskiyou*, two kinds of stills flourished during this time—commercial and hometown. Two of the larger distillers were wholesale dealers. Well hidden, they worked mostly at night so that they might not be detected, and bought sugar (the most important ingredient) in small quantities from various stores. Neither of these operations were ever raided. They sold their moonshine in 25-gallon barrels, supplying local saloons, barrooms, and speakeasies. Even general stores and markets sold the booze surreptitiously. Story has it that in Etna one of the local markets kept it inside a trap door near the cash register. Bottled in small canning jars, a customer could order a jar of hooch. Prices were fairly consistent, too, ranging from $1 to $3 a pint bottle.

Another well-known still was built near Orleans and run by Snabel. According to Bigelow, "He was finally raided and they took some of his whiskey and tested it. It was so darn good, they took 50 gallons to the hospital in Eureka and it was used for medicinal purposes."

There was a still run by the "goat man." Not only did he deliver goats to be butchered and cooked, he'd always delivered a quart or two of distilled whiskey when asked. One still in Seiad, run by Tom Edmondson, made whiskey commercially. When calling up to deliver a gallon, the caller would ask for an ox heart. If he wanted two gallons, he would ask for two ox hearts. Unfortunately,

Edmondson's still blew up, burning him seriously, but when he was arrested, he wasn't jailed. He was hospitalized—at the county's expense.

Many stills were located in the Klamath River area. One, run by a man named Riley, was located at Cinnabar Springs, where supplies were packed in by the Lester and Willis "Moon" Quigley mule train and whiskey was packed out. Others were located at Hamburg, Seiad, and Barkhouse Creek.

Julius Pereira, born and raised in Quartz Valley, was a boy during Prohibition. He noted, in the *1994 Siskiyou Pioneer*, that "every gulch had one operation it seemed."

"Pinky" Bill Mathews tells of his early adventures in Scott Valley during Prohibition. He remembers that "there was a still up every gulch and hollow, even in some of the old mines." As a young man, he and his buddies were occasionally hired to drive the cars used to haul Jackass whiskey. Pinky thought the adventure and money he earned were worth the risk, even when his father finally discovered him late one night. He said he got a pretty good blistering that time.

Incredibly, many people distilled whatever they could to produce alcohol during Prohibition years. According to George Wacker in the *1994 Siskiyou Pioneer*, Sterno, also called "canned heat," was occasionally distilled to separate out the denatured alcohol. Other alternatives to bootleg whiskey or moonshine was

WAGNER SALOON. Prohibition caused this popular Etna bar and many others to close their doors. (Courtesy Hayden Family Collection.)

vanilla extract or patent medicines. Extracts contained 35 percent alcohol (70-proof) and were cheap to buy. Many patent medicines contained at least 25 percent grain alcohol. And, of course, any sort of fruit was fermented for home use, especially pears and apples.

Violators were not treated well, but most stills were overlooked by local law enforcers. From 1922 through 1925, there were approximately 66 arrests for Prohibition violations. A few men were sent to San Quentin, but most of those convicted served anywhere from 30 days up to 500 days. Sometimes those days translated into dollars, meaning 30 days could equal $30 in fines. Only one woman was arrested.

One of the most intriguing stories of the early 1920s is that of Lillian Bounds. She is most noted for being "Mrs. Walt Disney" after her marriage in 1925. Born in 1898, she died in 1997. Although her biographies say she was born and raised in Idaho, she did live, at least for a time, in or near Fort Jones. She is a descendant of Frank Hooper of Hooperville and her mother was Jeanette Short, who died when Lillian was young. Her father, William Pehall Bounds, coincidentally was a traveling preacher who worked with the Native Americans of Idaho.

Pinky Mathews of Etna, aged 92, remembers Lillian. "She was a few years older than me but we both had reddish hair. Everyone liked her." Marie Piscantor, now deceased, often stated that she had had Lillian as one of her pupils. Marie taught at McAdams Creek School, but no class list or photos of Lillian in school could be located. Richard Luttrell, Fort Jones historian and a descendant of both the Hoopers and Shorts, recalls, "Of course, Lillian Bounds was Mrs. Walt Disney.

Map of Fort Jones Homes, 1900. The following are indicated: 1. J. Young house; 2. Dr. Cowan house; 3. early home of Lillian Bounds, Mrs. Walt Disney; 4. Lee Hodgkins house; 5. slaughter house; and 6. Davidson farm. (Courtesy Betty Hall–Irene Nelson Collection.)

She lived in Fort Jones for a time and her sister is buried in the Fort Jones Cemetery." Scanning the Fort Jones Cemetery records, there are two Bounds graves listed, one identified as Delia, the other unnamed. Jan Baker of Fort Jones recalls how her aunt (by marriage), the now-deceased Florence Baker, also spoke of and had correspondence with Lillian until recent years.

When Katie Bertleson of Etna, aged 99, was asked if she had ever heard of Lillian Bounds, her daughter asked, "Why does that name sound so familiar?" Katie replied, "Of course I knew her. She was Mrs. Walt Disney." The Cramer family of Moffett Creek also recalls that Walt Disney's nephew occasionally came to hunt deer on the Cramer ranch. And the roster of names for the Fort Jones Homecoming mailing list of 1984 lists Lillian Bounds Disney and her address in Burbank, California. Whatever her story, Mrs. Lillian Bounds Disney definitely has ties to the history of Hooperville and Fort Jones.

The 1920s and 1930s were decades of increasing social, political, and economic changes throughout Western Siskiyou County, and a time of real struggle for most rural families. During the Depression, many unemployed miners returned to abandoned mine sites and dredger operations to try to scratch out whatever kind of living they could.

By 1920, placer mining along the Klamath was nearly finished. Lode mines were replacing them. Mines like the Gray Eagle Mine up Indian Creek, near Happy Camp, opened up. This mine was worked during both World War I and World War II as the government subsidized the operation. Other mines to start up during this time included the Buzzard Hill Mine, Independence Mine, and Siskon Mine on Dillon Creek. The New York Mine on Indian Creek renewed activity around the Hooperville area, a boost for people struggling during the Depression.

Operations were often stopped or started depending upon finances and opportunity. Chrome mines were again being worked, providing opportunity for many local unemployed miners. According to Tuffy Fowler, the McBrooms along Salmon River packed chrome out of several local mines, loads as large as 300 to 350 pounds. Joe Richter packed out loads of chrome as well.

The timber and lumber industry more than doubled its production after 1900. Sawmills, which had primarily existed as a supplementary business to mining operations, took on greater importance. By 1920, a great number of mills were opening in response to increased world demand and higher prices. Several operators in Scott Valley reported increased production, namely George W. Brooks in Quartz Valley, W.M. Pinkerton at the southern end of Scott Valley, and the Wilson Brothers on Kidder Creek.

Also in 1920, C.J. Bergmann and E.W. Pereira of Scott Valley, representing the Forest Products Company and the Western Pine Lumber Company out of San Francisco, contracted for the entire season's output of several of the mills in the county. The lumber purchased was to be sent east where demand for western pine and fir lumber was growing. Bergmann also suggested the possibility of establishing a wooden box factory in Fort Jones. At the same time, Sunkist, who

MOUNTAIN ON FIRE. This 1926 photograph shows a footbridge across the Klamath River. (Courtesy U.S. Forest Service and Siskiyou County Museum.)

had found that wooden crates protected fruit from rotting better than anything else, bought a mill at Hilt and created Fruit Growers Supply Company. Sunkist also purchased every available piece of land in the region with timber. As a result, many hoped that such an enterprise would invite the construction of a railroad— a controversial and unlikely proposition. Nothing ever came of the box factory., and the railroad was never built in Scott Valley.

The USFS's presence increased after World War I. As the importance of natural resources and interest in unique lands grew, the government began to design policy and regulations relating to their protection. According to Jim McNeill, in the 1930s, the USFS began to shift from hiring only seasonal employees to hiring more permanent employees. Much of this came about because of the Depression. People had to work and programs were developed to put them to work.

In 1933, "from the normal buildup of 132 people, the Klamath had grown in the space of three months (from the time President Roosevelt had taken the President's Chair) to 900 CCC [Civilian Conservation Corps] enrollees, and to 90 Supervisory and Facilitating personnel in six camps." As a result, "grub stake fires," lit by those looking for temporary jobs as firefighters, dropped in number. Fire fighting became the primary focus of the service and there were a number of fires that brought attention to Siskiyou County's vast timber resources.

The Soap Creek Fire in 1927 and the Dillon Creek Fire in 1930 were two such fires. According to Jim McNeill, "The big Dillon fire . . . was really something. It took off on a crown. I guess one of the biggest crowns the Klamath has ever known. And it was really throwing up a world of smoke." One casualty of the fire was Roy England, who died when a snag knocked him down. During 1931, there was another rash of forest fires, including the Crawford Creek Fire. In 1935, the season started early (March 28), with fires on Mount Shasta and then around Western Siskiyou County. Fires continued well into the fall.

In 1929, Harry L. Englebright of Nevada City introduced a bill authorizing an appropriation of $4.5 million annually for 3 years and $4 million thereafter to create a fund to prevent fires in the federal forests. Government was encouraged to spend $1 to prevent fires rather than $3 to fight them. Even today, controversy abounds in regards to whether money is better spent preventing fires, by burning undergrowth earlier in the year, or fighting fires.

Agriculture continued to grow and develop all over the county in the years following World War I. In 1920, the *Siskiyou Standard* reported that the dairy industry in Scott Valley was "assuming considerable magnitude." The following operations were then listed as "intending to engage" or else "enlarging upon" leased acres for the year: Maggie Castro and W.C. Hammersley, 486 acres; M.T. Simas, 120 acres; A. Henriques, 100 acres; M. Neves and Sons Company, 200 acres; J.B. Davidson, 30 acres (to supply demand for horse feed needed by lumbering operations); and others "in prospect."

Most important was the technological advancement during this time. Tractors became more commonplace, replacing horses as the vehicle of choice. The machines certainly reduced the number of employees or ranch hands who worked on local ranches and farms.

In the early days, it was not uncommon for 20 men to board and work on a ranch. Today's ranches, of course, are worked with a minimum number of employees. For most operations, expenses nearly outstrip income, so that hiring more than one or two hands is generally not an option.

Another occupation that remained intact during the 1920s was packing. Though automobiles and trucks eventually traveled the rough and tumble roads, when weather turned bad, mules and pack trains returned as the link between the small river communities and the western valleys. Incredibly, a car was packed into Cecilville by John Nels McBroom in 1926. According to Bill Balfrey, McBroom's father

> also packed another car into the New River area below the old town of Denny, also in the 1920s. The cars were taken apart, but the frames had to be packed whole. At this time no roads were yet built leading into either town. A piano was packed over the Salmon Mountains and it was common to see 20 foot sections of hydraulic pipe or lumber being packed by the mules.

Bill Smith of Sawyer's Bar and Etna was a packer whose physical strength and stamina became almost legendary in Western Siskiyou County. On his back, he alone would carry the 100-pound side-hill slide that was needed to carve out the trail on the opposite side of the steep, snow-entrenched Salmon summit. And if required, he would pack the snow down with snowshoes, or "webs," if the animals bogged down. In Smith's own words:

> The county didn't keep the road open for us when we packed in. We had to do it ourselves. We put down 22-foot pipe and we'd dump coal down through it and then drop powder down in there and blast that snow so it would melt out faster. We tunneled at the summit three different times.

On heavier loads, several packers would go in a mile or so ahead and set up an A-frame with block-and-tackle. The loads would be lifted off the backs of the tired mules and loaded back on to fresh mules. "Some of the mules would trot when they saw the A-frame." The winters of 1926 and 1932 were fierce ones. Snow accumulated on the mountain so deeply that tunnels had to be carved out. The tunnels were large enough for automobiles to pass through. Smith reveled in the fact that he could "load a mule a minute," after the bell boy placed the saddles on the animals' backs. The Salmon River Diamond Hitch was the common knot, still used by experienced packers today.

BILL SMITH. Smith and partner J. Ahlgren negotiate a sled down from the summit in the 1920s. (Courtesy Siskiyou County Museum.)

George W. Smith, who had contracted to haul mail over the Salmon summit, bought Snowden, which he then used as a resting spot for his packers and mules. There were two pack trains, one going each way, from Etna to Snowden. The town of Snowden burned down in the early summer of 1935, destroying everything but a small cabin. It was later sold to Robert and Betty Young and, today, Steve and Martha Lindgren of Fort Jones own it.

Around 1920, Bill Smith and his father, whose company was called G.W. Smith and Sons Auto and Stage Company, began using trucks to go over and back over Salmon Mountain, and it wasn't long before Cats were used to clear the deep snow during winter. The first two trucks the Smiths got were Republics (a $3/4$-ton and 1-ton). The third and fourth trucks were Whites. In the end, "We had five Whites, two Dodge screen sides—just pickups—and a one ton GMC truck." In Bill's words, "We had a contract for 16 years, and it was just two days that we didn't get the mail through."

Curtis Fowler and his brothers, along with partner John Ahlgren, packed for 20 years out of Callahan. Some of their packing expeditions included hauling Christmas trees in 1947 and packing in tins of fry (Rainbow, Eastern Brook, and German Brown) to the upper mountain lakes. They packed in stoves and equipment for miners such as Alex Bouvier, and even hauled in loads of beaver, which were being reintroduced into several mountain areas. Making a penny a pound, that equalled $2 for a 200-pound load. During the Depression, however, that was welcome money.

Pack trains continued into the 1930s when Charlie Snapp took over the mail contract to Sawyer's Bar and Salmon River country. In 1938 he retired the mule trains and began employing snow cats as the best means to push aside snow on the mountain passes and roads.

Unfortunately, this increased mechanization in farming, hauling, and lumbering, as well as the diminished opportunities for mining, left many men hard-pressed for work in northern California. Many returned to "scratch" mining, whether dredging the rivers on small floating dredges or digging through the old mining sites long abandoned by prospectors. Abandoned mining shacks became homes to those too poor to pay for room or board. Many locals recall their fathers or grandfathers "eking" out a living this way.

Hobos became a common sight. According to many old-timers, men came knocking on doors, begging for any kind of work. Filling in for a day or a week or a month, they were fed well, but paid little. Sometimes these men moved on only to return the next year when haying season or farming season approached. Only a few settled permanently, most of those associated with work on the big dredges scattered through the county.

The Civilian Conservation Corps (CCC), created to provide work for young men, was a popular program in Western Siskiyou County during the 1930s. Several camps were established in Seiad, Scott Bar, Indian Creek, Clear Creek, Callahan, and at various other points around the region. Crews were used to construct roads, such as the Baldy Mountain Road from Greenhouse to the

Hanson Ranch and the Indian Creek Road between the south Fork of Indian Creek Bridge and Classic Hill, or on water works projects, such as one in Callahan. Men also worked on mining operations, such as hydraulic mining at Scott Bar. Most of all, the CCCs helped to repress fires.

The 1920s and 1930s impacted the Native American families in the region even more severely. Many were already struggling to survive on seasonal jobs. Added to this hardship was the accepted policy of sending Native American children off to special schools far from home where they were separated from family and cultural traditions. One such Shasta local was Fred Wicks Jr., who was sent to Sherman Institute, an "Indian" school in southern California. While there, however, he met Nina Kintano, a Cahuilla girl. After graduation, they married and moved home to Scott Valley.

One evening, as Nina and Fred discussed the poor conditions facing local Native American families, Fred talked about the treaty that had never been ratified and the notion of a reservation first proposed in 1851 and again in 1874. With Nina's encouragement, he soon found that the Indian Reorganization Act of June 18, 1934 could provide an answer. He made trips to Sacramento in the hope of establishing a reservation in Scott Valley.

Rialto and Nellie (Bryan) Burton, at first reluctant to sell, eventually sold land to the tribe for a reservation; in 1927 they sold 364 acres for $20,000 and later an

INDIAN CREEK CCC CAMP. This road crew, under the direction of Ernest Roberts, was photographed c. 1933 at Indian Creek Camp F21. (Courtesy U.S. Forest Service and Siskiyou County Museum.)

QUARTZ VALLEY RESERVATION. From left to right are (children in front) Tom Webster; Betty Wicks; and Valentina Harrie; (back row) Mr. Gallagher; Fred L. and Nina Wicks; Mary, Barbara, and Harry Burcell; Hazel Harrie; Bill Patterson; Fred Wicks; and Jetty Thom. (Courtesy Betty Hall Collection.)

additional 240 acres. In the meantime, Fred set about gathering names of all the Shasta families. The Quartz Valley Upper Klamath Shasta Indian Reservation was established and the constitution ratified on June 15, 1939. At that time, there was only enough land for 13 allotments. As the list was revised, the Bureau of Indian Affairs decided that the Native Americans most needy, regardless of tribe, would receive the allotments. When a Karuk family claiming ancestry as Upper Klamath was added to the list, many Shasta families withdrew their applications.

That many of his people would not participate was a bitter pill for Fred to swallow. At least his father, Fred Wicks Sr., had received one of the first assignments. Then Fred was dealt another blow. Because he was only one-quarter Shasta, he was ineligible to receive an allotment under the bureau's policy of "one-half Indian only" eligibility. A letter was sent from Washington, D.C. to Mr. Boggus, the Indian agent, demanding that Fred be given an assignment as his wife was full-blooded and his daughter more than half. After the reservation was established, the membership officially adopted Fred Wicks as a tribal member and his assignment was granted.

Ironically, as a result of the California Rancheria (Termination) Act of August 18, 1958, the Quartz Valley reservation was closed. Members holding allotments were given title to their land. A class action lawsuit, known as the Tillie-Hardwick

HAULING CHRISTMAS TREES. Curtis Fowler and his brother pack out trees near Upper Mill Creek outside Callahan in 1947. The brothers packed out trees from 1932 to 1950. (Courtesy Tuffy Fowler Collection.)

case, was filed on behalf of all reservations terminated in 1956. Finally, in 1982, Tillie-Hardwick was settled and all reservations, including the Quartz Valley reservation, were reestablished. Only four original assignees are still living: Anthony Jerry, Richard Sargeant, Arlene Harrie, and Roy Hall.

Another Native American to make headlines during this time was Johnny Southard, who ran in the "Indians only" great Redwood Highway Marathon of 1927. Begun as a publicity stunt to bring tourism to the newly constructed Redwood Highway, there was a $5,000 prize awaiting the winner. Of the 36 national runners, 5 were from Siskiyou County. Mr. H.G. Boorse of Happy Camp helped to sponsor the local runners and quickly took up a publicity campaign. "He gave his runners what he fancied to be Indian names," said Johnny Southard, a Karuk living in Happy Camp, who became known as "Mad Bull." His brother Marion was "Fighting Stag" and his brother Gorham was "Rushing Water." Another local was Henry Thomas, renamed "Flying Cloud." A fifth runner was James McNeill from Hornbrook, who was called "Great White Deer." His sponsor was H.B. Littler and Company, the west coast representative for Durante Motors Company.

Every race needs a queen and Miss Dorothy Allen, a Karuk from Orleans, easily won the competition. She was called "Princess Little Fawn." In order to generate world interest, a well-known runner, Joe LaFontaine from Canada, was entered. There was also talk that some Yaqui runners from Old Mexico would compete and, from what Jim McNeill heard, they "could run 600 or 700 miles on a handful of parched corn."

While many of the others had to go into intense training for the race, Southard kept on running the hills around Happy Camp and ran 60 miles each day, from Happy Camp, over Cade Mountain to Hamburg, and back to Happy Camp.

The runners gathered at the Civic Center in San Francisco on June 14, 1927. Reporters, celebrities, and movie cameras were everywhere. Governor Jimmie Rolf and San Francisco mayor Angelo Rossi were late, but when they arrived, they presented each of the runners with two letters in a pouch to hang around their necks. The runners were instructed to deliver the letters from the governor of California and the mayor of San Francisco to the governor of Oregon and the mayor of Grants Pass, Oregon, a "mere" 482.5 miles away.

Along the way, towns posted local prize money to be awarded the first racer to reach their town. In Santa Rosa, Flying Cloud picked up $50. While Flying Cloud slept in Santa Rosa, Mad Bull passed him and picked up the envelope in Garberville. There was $35 inside. In Fortuna, he won $100; in Eureka, another $100; and another $100 in Crescent City. Mad Bull didn't use the cot provided by the support car or the doctor that kept close tabs on the runners. He made 60 miles a day and slept in a hotel or "auto park," as motels were called in those days, each night. One young boy in Eureka wondered why Mad Bull didn't wear a feather headdress or "flourish a tomahawk." The boy, Garth Sanders, later became a reporter for the *Record Searchlight* in Redding, California. He interviewed Southard in 1976.

SNOW TUNNEL ON SALMON. This 1932 photograph shows a tunnel on top of Salmon Mountain. (Courtesy Betty Young Collection.)

PUSHING SNOW. A "Cat" was used to push snow off the Salmon Mountain Summit Road in the 1940s. (Courtesy Betty Young Collection.)

McNeill trailed behind and when he reached San Rafael, where the runners were crowded together, a woman, "in a Cadillac as long as from here to there" knocked him to the ground. He was checked out at the local hospital and, after two and a half hours, was allowed to return to the race. Meanwhile, Mad Bull and Flying Cloud were eating up the miles. At Gasque, a Warner Brothers automobile carrying Myrna Loy pulled up alongside McNeill and asked if he'd pose with Myrna. She wanted McNeill's hand around her shoulders, but his hands were dirty. She told him she'd wear the dirty blouse when McNeill came to Hollywood so he could "pick me out from all the other pretty girls."

Though McNeill didn't come in first, he did finish the race in a very long 8 days, 2 hours, and 10 minutes. Flying Cloud made the journey in 7 days and 22 hours, but that was 8 hours too late for the $5,000 cup of gold. He returned home to Happy Camp, still a winner in the eyes of his people. In the end, Johnny Southard, now known to the world as Mad Bull, crossed the finish line in Grants Pass, unchallenged, on June 22 to finish what he called "the greatest day of my life." Fewer than one-third of the starters completed the race, so for local boys to take first, second, and fifth place was a point of civic pride.

On the heels of the Great Depression came World War II. For many people, this was a way out of poverty and a way to make a decent living. Some of the local boys joined up as soon as they could; others waited to be drafted.

One family deeply affected by the war was the Starr family of Scott Valley. Four brothers entered different branches of the armed services. All four, thankfully, returned home. Technical Sergeant Kenneth Starr served in the 191st Field Artillery, 560th Ordinancy Tank Maintenance Company. He spent two and a half years overseas, first in France, then Belgium, and then Germany. Corporal J. Vernon Starr served in the 850th Engineers, and worked on building and maintaining airports in England and France. He was a member of the D-Day invasion. Staff Sergeant Lewis Fred Starr was a ball turret gunner, or belly gunner, in the 8th Air Force, 381st Bomb Squadron. He flew 35 missions, many over Germany. One very close call he had was when a bomb "got stuck and no one wanted to manually release it." Fred freed it by using a screwdriver and the bomb dropped on a small village, destroying it completely. Medals awarded L. Fred Starr included the Distinguished Flying Cross and the Air Medal. Seaman Second Class Gerald "Gyp" Starr was the youngest of the four brothers. He served on the

WORLD WAR II SOLDIERS. Fred and Clay Fleck of Scott Valley were photographed during the war. (Courtesy Mike Bryan Family Collection.)

U.S.S. *Iowa Battleship* from 1945 to 1946, but he also re-entered active duty and served in the 24th Infantry, 19th Infantry Regiment (Fox Company), of the United States Army during the Korean War.

Norman "Buzz" Helm, who lied about his age and left high school to enlist, served as a corporal in the 32nd Infantry, 7th Division, 24th Corps, under General Douglas MacArthur during the last days of World War II. Buzz finally returned to receive his high school diploma from Etna High School in 2000. Delores Hottendorf, specialist first class, served as an intelligence cryptographer with the Second Group Waves in Washington, DC during World War II. She worked on decoding messages from the South Pacific. Several who were lost during the war included William Besoain; Arthur Case; Norman Eastlick; James Mathews, who was killed in the D-Day invasion at Normandy; Jack Norris; Donald Pinkerton; and Eugene Rivallier.

On May 18, 1947, the Etna Women's Club dedicated three memorial trees and a plaque in honor of those who had died in the war. Three men fallen in battle and honored at the celebration included Raymond Marx, Robert Jacobi, and Bernard Tucker. The dedication of the plaque was carried out by the Veterans of Foreign Wars, including Malcolm Hayden (the first combatant to survive a crash landing on the surface of the water), Minor Cross, Norman Short, Kenneth Short, Emmet Draper, Walter Mathews, and Gerald Naylor.

Included here are more names, but most likely, not every soldier's name is listed: Bobby Young, Tom Tickner, and Wes Andrews from Scott Valley, who all fought in the Battle of the Bulge; Jess Fowler and Melvin Cramer of Callahan; Leroy Ward of Happy Camp; N. Malcolm Hayden of Etna; Sergeant Frances George of Greenview; Captain James Bailey of Seiad, who received the Distinguished Flying Cross; Lieutenant Bob Jensen from Oak Bar, who received the Air Medal, Four Oak Leaf Cluster, and Distinguished Flying Cross; Technical Sergeant Leland Custer of Oro Fino, who was wounded in battle; Robert Bunker of Fort Jones; Private Alonso Mullin of Etna; Corporal Hubert Mullin of Greenview, who served with Patton in Africa, Sicily, and Italy; Grand Master Third Class Tom Clyburn of Klamath River; Staff Sergeant Mike Skeahan from Klamath River, who fought in the Battle of the Bulge; Master Sergeant Bob Thompson of Klamath River; Grand Master Second Class Bob White of Klamath River; Grand Master Third Class Woody Clyburn from Klamath River, who was wounded at Guadalcanal; Bob DeAvilla of Klamath River; Master Sergeant Jessie Frances of Klamath River; Private First Class Delos Levulett from Horse Creek, who received the Bronze Star; Sergeant First Class Earl Godfrey of Etna; Staff Sergeant Charles Dillman of Etna; Captain Charles Ramsey from Sawyer's Bar, who received the Distinguished Flying Cross, Air Medal, and 13 Oak Leaf Cluster; Corporal Larry Borba of Etna; Staff Sergeant Virgil Nesbitt from Scott Bar; Master Sergeant Forest Winters of Fort Jones; Corporal James Branson of Fort Jones; Corporal Donald Messner of Fort Jones; Private Ralph Smith from Etna, who received the Combat Infantry Badge; Corporal Jack Timmons of Etna; Master Sergeant Robert Humphreys from Happy Camp; Private First Class Bud

McNeal Jr. from Forks of Salmon, who received the Bronze Star; Private First Class Harold Marx from Etna, who received the Bronze Star; Private First Class James Wolford of Etna, who was wounded; Corporal Neil Fox from Fort Jones; Kenneth Eller, in the Army under Patton; Don Brazil, who served in the Navy during the Berlin Conflict; George Brookshire, USMC, 1942–1945; Harold Deppen Glider, a mechanic in the Army Air Corps, 1943–1946; Marjorie Lewandowski, Women's Royal Navy; Edward Lewandowski, U.S.S. Patrol Craft 462, 1942–1945; Howard Savage, who served in the Navy, 1944–1946; Ruel Marx, USMC, 1941–1945; Raymond Marx, Army Air Force, 1941–1945; Gene Crawford, who served in the Army in the European Theatre, 1941–1945; George Eastlick, who was at Pearl Harbor and received the Purple Heart; Paul Garrison, Navy; and Oliver Johnson, Army Air Force.

Joining up during the last six months of the war, or later, were Joe DeFaria, Joe Eller, Joe Lewis, Joe Valin, and Bill King, all of Scott Valley. Earl W. Carlson from Etna, seaman apprentice of the U.S. Navy, entered the service in 1951.

STEAM TRACTOR. This Case tractor, owned by Clarence Dudley of Etna, was photographed hauling lumber in Callahan beyond Rodney Gregg's place in the 1930s. (Courtesy Siskiyou County Museum.)

6. The Following Decades

Following the war, many people were anxious to return to their old lives. For others, life would never be the same, particularly after contact with the larger world had enlarged their perception. As in rural areas all over the United States, the war had opened the door to new industries and a more mobile population. Preservation of Western Siskiyou's past and its traditions, however, remained as strong as ever.

Ranching continued to thrive in the years following World War II. In 1954, the Siskiyou County Cattlemen's Association, in an effort to recognize improvements or accomplishments in breeding programs as well as for conservation and farming practices, adopted a "Cattleman of the Year" award. The first Cattleman of the Year, selected in 1955, was Nerva M. Hayden of Etna. Born in 1892 in the Callahan's Ranch Hotel, he was one of four children. Hayden married Gladys Jenner in 1916, and the couple bought the old Hans Hansen Ranch in partnership with Frank S. Jenner, Gladys's father. The Hayden ranch eventually became one of the largest in Western Siskiyou County, as well as one of the primary rangeland permittees, running cattle in the area of Little North Fork. Other early Western Siskiyou Cattlemen of the Year included Clarence Dudley, 1958, and Charles F. Hammond, 1962. The Siskiyou County Cattlemen's Association still recognizes a Cattleman of the Year each fall. In conjunction, the Siskiyou County Cattlewomen's Association recognizes a "Cowbelle of the Year."

One endeavor was the construction of the Fort Jones Museum in 1947. A unique structure, this small but fascinating building was erected by William T. Davidson, George Milne, Harry Bryan, Arland Walker, and Eddie Edgecomb, all members of original pioneer families or residents of the area. Its outside walls are plastered with mill stones, Native American rocks and tools, an enormous piece of obsidian and other rock samples, even a couple cannon balls from the old fort. Visitors love to walk the length of the museum, studying its variety and history.

Elsie (Nelson) Hill designed the collection exhibits, as well as catalogued and marked the early donations. The museum's list of exhibits includes one of the west's most outstanding basket collections, perhaps even the largest collection. Another unusual exhibit, the one children enjoy most, is a two-headed calf born on the Con Mulloy ranch outside Fort Jones. In 1954, the museum was enlarged and new cases installed. Plans are in motion for a 2003 addition as well.

The Shasta Rain Rock, sitting on the north side of the building, has been the object of much publicity over the years and is one of the most fascinating aspects of the museum. It was discovered in April 1948 when a state road crew, working to widen the Klamath River highway near Gottsville, California, uncovered a strange-looking boulder. The boulder, a 2-ton chunk of soapstone, is 4 to 5 feet long, 3 feet across, and stands 2 feet high. Its surface is covered with more than 70 deep pocks and holes, some as wide as a fist. There are also many scratches and carvings. For several years, the Rain Rock had a companion, a 500- to 1,000-pound piece of "Happy Camp" jade. Unfortunately, one night, the jade disappeared without a trace.

The Shasta believe that to leave the Rain Rock uncovered causes a hard winter and to disturb the stone can cause disaster. Story has it that the stone was buried by the Shasta in the late 1800s to halt the severe winters they had been having. Some speculate that it could have been the winter of 1860 to 1861 when floods and torrential rains devastated Western Siskiyou County.

The Rain Rock has also become world famous. When a heavyweight fight at Madison Square Garden had to be canceled for two nights in a row, a telegram was sent to Fort Jones requesting that the rock be covered. The request was granted and the bout went on as clouds, but no rainfall, filled the skies above New York.

SHASTA RAIN ROCK. Uncovered in 1948 by a Fort Goff road crew, it now sits alongside the Fort Jones Museum. (Courtesy MaryLou Slette.)

There have been some other intriguing events associated with the Rain Rock. In the 1980s, a local logging truck pulled up to weigh in on the scales located next door to the museum. As it pulled away, one log rolled off and hit the Rain Rock, shaking it on its pedestal. The next night, 3 feet of fresh powdered snow fell over most of Scott Valley. Though it may have seemed coincidental to some people, others noted that there had been no storm warnings, and the date was April 1.

One of the western county's most popular entertainments, the annual Scott Valley Pleasure Park Association Rodeo, had its start in the late 1940s. The outgrowth of an earlier polo club initiated by Jim Mathews, who died in the war, it wasn't long before the group needed more space. It was George "Dad" Dillman who provided a good-sized chunk of land for an arena and, soon, the idea of holding a rodeo took hold. Others involved in the creation of the Pleasure Park Association and the first rodeos included Fred Brown, Frank Bryan, Bib Dillman, Pinky Mathews, and Fred Wolford. Election of officers took place in 1948 and the first rodeo was held in May 1949. At first, stock was provided by local ranchers, but the rodeo's popularity continued to grow and eventually it became a professional rodeo. Today, it marks one of the first weekends of the California rodeo circuit with an attendance of more than 4,000 spectators. A second rodeo, dubbed the Old-Timer's Rodeo, was added to the list of the association's activities in 1976; this year's July event marks the 26th annual rodeo put on entirely by locals with local stock. An array of unusual events, including the Wild-Cow Milking Contest, the Saddle Cow Race and the Cowhide Race, as well as the Kids' Mutton-Bustin' and others, head the list. The Pleasure Park Association also sponsors a Junior Pleasure Park Drill Team, where young riders come and ride, then perform as one of the rodeo's main attractions. The May weekend's activities also include a dance, a pancake breakfast sponsored by the Etna Lions' Club, a parade through Etna, and other activities provided by local organizations.

Baseball continued to be a popular community sport. One person influential in the development of baseball in Scott Valley was Fred Ruff. He played the sport in his early days and supported youth baseball throughout his life. In one game during high school, Ruff managed to strike out 21 batters against Etna; he would have had 22, but his catcher dropped the third strike. Out of high school, Fred signed on with the Oakland Oaks, a minor league affiliated with the Oakland Athletics, but did not accept the position.

In 1950, the first game played by an All-Star team in a Nor-Cal league took place. Members of the Scott Valley Stars that year included Wilbur Facey, Kenny Simpson, Don Purdy, George Bell, Neil Evans, Albert Facey, Ken Short, Fred Ruff, Ernie Bigham, Duane Glendenning, Don Duncan, Pete Storti, and manager Smiley Guerin. In Happy Camp and the surrounding area, Leonard Shelton was instrumental in establishing baseball leagues for kids. Today his widow, Helen Doggett Shelton (whose family settled Doggett Creek), his daughters, and his grandchildren still play and support baseball in Western Siskiyou County.

The Siskiyou Golden Fair is now the most significant and popular event in Siskiyou County. Attended by more than 50,000 people annually, it is held during

ETNA MUSEUM. Maintained by NDGW, Eschschotzia Parlor No. 112, the Etna Museum on Main Street was recently enlarged and remodeled. Shown are Thelma Mills and Bernita Tickner. (Courtesy Gail Jenner Collection.)

the first full week of August. Not only a social event, it is a cultural one, with arts and crafts exhibits, 4-H and Future Farmers of America animal and project exhibits, horse competitions, a rodeo, a variety of musical concerts, and a carnival. Heralded as one of California's best county fairs, it contributes substantially to Yreka's economy.

In 1949, Siskiyou County celebrated the 100th anniversary of the original "forty-niners" with an exhibit at the State Fair at Sacramento that was then taken to the Los Angeles County Fair. Elsie Evelyn (Nelson) Hill wrote the verse characterizing the exhibit's theme: "SISKIYOU COUNTY—THE MINER CAME FOR GOLD—HE STAYED TO TILL THE SOIL—BEHOLD—HE SAW GREAT FORESTS—AND RIVERS TOO—THIS IS THE WEALTH OF—SISKIYOU." The exhibit was made up of lumber products, gold pans holding agricultural products, and even pieces of the county's $1-million gold collection that is still displayed at the Yreka courthouse under glass.

The 1950s opened up with the Korean War. Many who had been too young to fight during World War II enlisted in the armed services in the years following. One of Scott Valley's twentieth century heroes was Glenn Hall, a member of the Shasta Nation. It all started so unceremoniously.

On the afternoon of July 6, 1948, H. Chester "Chet" McBroom and Bill Martin were headed to Yreka to enlist in the army when they spotted Glenn Hall, a friend,

ETNA POLO CLUB. Established in the late 1930s, the club included members such as, from left to right, Hearst Dillman, Bernie Tucker, Buster Naegle, Charlie Dillman, Curtis Fowler, and Frank Bryan. Jim Matthews was an original member. (Courtesy Tuffy Fowler Collection.)

hitchhiking back from Yreka. The three went on to Yreka and signed up, first Chet, then Glenn, then Bill. Chet said, "Our numbers were only one apart. Mine was 19325773, Glenn's was 19325774 and Bill's was 19325775. We were part of I Company, 4th Infantry Division."

After basic training was over, the friends parted. Glenn joined the 82nd Airborne. Private McBroom was sent to Honolulu and worked in the U.S. Army Pacific post office. "We handled all the mail coming in and going out for the entire Pacific." He spent his last two years back at Fort Ord in California administering aptitude tests. "I gave from six-hundred to a thousand tests a day. I gave tests to lots of the locals, too: Gyp Star, Ben Tozier, and Bob Smith, and they all passed." He was discharged in 1951.

Glenn Hall was killed in Korea and received the Distinguished Service Medal for personally "wiping out two machine gun nests and holding the enemy at bay until his unit could hold a secure position." In Korea, Glenn quickly rose to the rank of corporal. He was a favorite among his division. When he was wounded in a skirmish, he was told he would be shipped home, but he refused, saying he needed to get back to his unit.

The rest is best told by those who were with Glenn in Korea:

> General Orders, Order 420, from the HEADQUARTERS EIGHTH UNITED
> STATES ARMY KOREA (EUSAK), Office of the Commanding General
> APO 301. Dated 10 June 1951. Distinguished-service Cross
> (Posthumous)—Award. Section I:
>
> I. AWARD OF THE DISTINGUISHED-SERVICE CROSS (POSTHUMOUS)—
> By direction of the President, under the provisions of the Act of
> Congress, approved 9 July 1918 (WD Bul 43, 1918), and pursuant to
> authority contained in AR 600-45, the Distinguished-Service Cross, for
> extraordinary heroism in action is awarded posthumously in the name
> of the Commander-in-Chief, Far East, to the following-named enlisted
> man:
>
> Corporal GLENN M. HALL, RA19325774, Infantry, United States
> Army. Corporal HALL, a member of the 1st Ranger Company,
> (Airborne), 2nd Infantry Division, distinguished himself by
> extraordinary heroism in action against the enemy near Chipyong-ni,
> Korea. At approximately 0300 hours on the morning of 15 February
> 1951, the 1st Platoon of the company, of which Corporal HALL was a

*THE PLEASURE PARK
PARADE. The parade is part of
the annual Scott Valley May
Rodeo. Pictured is Grand
Marshal George Dillman
carrying the flag. (Courtesy Liz
Dillman-Bowen Collection.)*

JAKE HAYDEN, BRONC RIDER. Pictured at the annual Scott Valley Pleasure Park Association May Rodeo, Jake, the son of Rick and Cheryl Hayden of Callahan, rides a bareback bronc. (Courtesy Liz Dillman-Bowen Collection.)

member, was given the mission of attacking and securing a hill from which friendly forces had been driven by the enemy. As the attack commenced, Corporal HALL, a light machine gunner in the platoon, emplaced his weapon in an exposed position from which he furnished cover-carbine, Corporal HALL moved up the hill under intense enemy fire to join his comrades and aid them in the assault. When the platoon reached the crest of the hill, Corporal HALL was instructed to contact the unit on the flank of the platoon. Moving out under heavy enemy mortar and small-arms fire, he proceeded to the knoll supposedly held by the adjacent friendly unit and found it occupied by enemy troops entrenched in foxholes. Assaulting one of the foxholes, he succeeded in killing the enemy occupying it, then used the position as cover against enemy grenade and rifle fire. In the course of the fighting at this position, Corporal HALL was wounded by an enemy grenade; however, he tenaciously held the position, inflicting heavy casualties on the enemy, forcing them to fall back and single-handedly securing the flank of his platoon. The selfless devotion to duty and extraordinary heroism displayed by Corporal HALL reflected great credit on himself and were in keeping with the highest traditions of military service. Entered the federal services from California.

Glenn Hall was shipped home and buried in the Fort Jones Cemetery where he was given full military honors.

In 1989, the remaining living members of the 1st Ranger Company (Airborne) gathered at the Fort Jones Cemetery with Glenn Hall's family and friends for a dedication ceremony. The Rangers presented a plaque and headstone designed for placement on all company member graves. Glenn was to receive the first plaque, for, as every member of the Rangers present stated, "Glenn was our hero." When the Rangers left Fort Jones, they were to travel across the United States to visit every burial site of their deceased.

Other Korean, Vietnam, and present-day veterans include the following: Dave Neasbitt, USMC; Don Purdy, Merchant Marines; Ronald Sargent, Air Force; Harold Slette, Army (awarded Purple Heart); Jim Butler, Army (107th Ordinance); Wayne Potter, Navy; George Meek, Army; Charles McDonald;

GLENN HALL, AIRBORNE RANGER. *A local hero who died in Korea, Hall was posthumously awarded the Distinguished Service Cross. (Courtesy Betty Hall–Irene Nelson Collection.)*

WINTER OF 1955. With snow levels doubled, the winter of 1955 stranded many. Note the roof-high drifts in early December. (Courtesy Betty Young Collection.)

Danny Daniels, Air Force; Herb Janney, Army; Dick Romney, Army; Larry Borba, Army; Don Glendenning, Air Force; Jim J. Johnson, USMC; Bob Ferrier; Joe Hurlimann, Army; Chet McFall, Army Air Force (Japan and Guam); Dan Martin, Army (1967–1969); John Deppen, Army (1958–1963); Kirk Deppen, Army Combat Engineer (1969–1971); John "Butch" Munson, Army (1965–1967); Stan Maplesden, Army (Vietnam); Clint Custer, 101st (Vietnam); E. "Butch" Bigham, Army (Vietnam); Ed Stone (Vietnam); Richard Moore (Vietnam); Norbert Rowe, Navy (1968–1972); Richard Forde, Navy (1964); Jim W. Smith, Army (1958–1962); Wayne Meek, Air Force (1948–1952); Gary Prince, USMC (1967–1968); Fred Giordano, Navy SeaBees (1968–1969), and Navy Seals (1970); Craig Campbell; Dan Spallino, Army; Brad Spallino, Army; Clint Newton, Army; Arely Valadez, Navy; Lee Nober, USMC and Army in Korea and Vietnam; Tom Gephart, Army; Jack Smith, Army; Ken Berry, Army (127th Military Police); Steven Dillman, Army (Warrant Officer); Patrick Dillman, Army; Carver Hugh Gepford; Mark Gepford; George Gephart, Army Rangers (Grenada, 1976–present); Jason Deppen (1992–1997); Belinda Naylor, Air Force; Jason Hope, USMC; Melinda Ford, Army; Gary Spallino; Sargent Wook McBroom (Kosovo); Jonathan Varnell, Air Force; Albert Denny, Army helicopter mechanic (1968–1971); Barry Folendorf, Army; and Gary Folendorf, Army.

In December 1997, the oldest living U.S. Postal Service mail carrier, Charlie Snapp, a Shasta Indian from Etna, was honored with a stamp made in his image. It was the only time in U.S. Postal Service history that anyone has been distinguished by having a stamp designed, or "cut," before dying first. The reason: more than 75 years of continued, even heroic service.

Born on October 22, 1903, Charlie, like so many men of his day, worked a variety of jobs. But it was around 1918, when he was just 15 years old, that he began carrying the mail, first with routes to Medford, Gazelle, Callahan, and Etna. Later, he began hauling the mail over Salmon Mountain. Like the stalwart packer Bill Smith before him, Charlie's greatest challenge was weather, especially unpredictable snowstorms. Over the years, he wore out several mailbags and his daughter Helen Lincoln still cherishes the last bag he carried. As a child, she often accompanied him on his route, recalling that one snowy day she rode on the sled clutching the groceries they were hauling—along with the mail—to the Forks of Salmon. Charlie towed her and the loaded sled over Salmon Mountain with a Cat. Suddenly, the sled cut loose and Helen went racing down the steep slope until she ran into a tree. "I had eggs in my hair but the mail was fine."

There were several times when people tried to rob Charlie on the long trip to Forks of Salmon. They usually parked their cars in the road. On one occasion, a logging truck also came by and Charlie, having spotted the would-be thieves, told the truck driver to "run them off the road." Charlie always prided himself on the fact that none of the robbery attempts were successful.

SALMON RIVER, WINTER 1964. *After rainfall topped three times normal amounts, flood water washed away much of Siskiyou County. Wert's Gas Station, at McNiel Creek, was nearly swept into the river. (Courtesy McBroom Family Collection.)*

135

In the first years of hauling, Charlie packed a mule in good weather and a sled in bad. In the 1930s, he got his first diesel-powered Cat that easily dragged his sled over the Salmon summit. Later, he used trucks, which he wore out, and in his final years, his son Ernie drove him. Charlie, however, still packed the mail. In all, he spent more than 75 years loading, packing, and delivering the mail, regardless of weather or road conditions—an honor no other American has ever held.

Because he was so well known and reliable, Charlie often hauled groceries or medicine, in addition to the mail, to the residents along Salmon River. Moreover, because he spoke the native languages, the old Indians who still didn't speak English (or refused to) would stop Charlie and tell him what groceries and other items they wanted. The Karuk called him "Wa-po-hetch," which means "nice boy, favorite boy."

In 1968, Charlie was given his first citation by the U.S. Postal Service for his many years of service. Then, in 1997, he was honored with a plaque displaying the new stamp in his image, but because there is a law that does not allow stamps to be released until several years after an individual's death, the official Charlie Snapp stamp will not be released until some time in the future. Charlie died on January 25, 2001 at the age of 97. But many remember him and talk of his faithful and tireless dedication to doing a job well done.

SCOTT VALLEY, WINTER 1964. The Scott River Bridge was ripped away during the floods of 1964. (Courtesy Tuffy Fowler Collection.)

SLIDE ALONG SALMON RIVER. The Salmon River Road was destroyed by a slide about one-half mile upstream from Tripp Point. (Courtesy Siskiyou County Museum.)

As in so many other out-of-the-way places, the hippie movement took Western Siskiyou County by storm in the 1960s. People flocked from the cities, ready to live near nature, some only to find that living the natural way meant long hours of work and plenty of ingenuity. With so much rural land available at reasonable prices, and with neighbors who believed in a live-and-let-live philosophy, new communes quickly grew to 100 persons or more. One community bought the Black Bear Mine in Salmon River from Mr. Dysert. Even actor Peter Coyote lived there, if only for a little while.

Many old-timers, who grew up during the Depression and two world wars, taught these "city folk" how things used to be. With much hard work, many of the newcomers learned to live off the land. Water wheels, solar panels, and other alternatives to electric power made life, if not simpler, certainly more interesting. Mike DeFaria, a miner from the Salmon River area who had been gold mining for most of his life, quickly became a friend and mentor to those eager to learn. He once said, "I don't live like them. They learned how to live like me."

Controversy has always seemed to surround Western Siskiyou County, perhaps because it attracts individuals who are single minded and hard working, whether they are to the right or left politically. And in an area populated by roughly 12,000 people, everyone who wants to express an opinion is heard—loud and clear. The

INDIAN RIDGE BURN. Two Forest Service personnel take stock of the extent of burned area after the 1959 blaze. (Courtesy U.S. Forest Service and Siskiyou County Museum.)

creation of the wilderness area in the Marble Mountains was just such a hotbed of controversy. Ranchers were assured that a "Wilderness" designation would not infringe upon their 80-year-old grazing permits. Indeed, cattle assist in fire repression and the USFS has begun to recognize their importance in keeping fine fuel to a minimum.

When the Wilderness designation was approved, locals had no choice but to accept the decision. Those who had always ridden to the mountains on horseback continued as before, but the mule and horse packers had not anticipated how many would come to "see" the new wilderness. It wasn't long before horses had to sidestep enthusiastic backpackers. The preserve encompasses 220,000 acres, including 87 glacier lakes. There are also 20 species of conifer, including the rare Brewer's spruce.

The BigFoot Scenic Byway is another opportunity for visitors to see the more remote portions of Western Siskiyou County. A stretch of 85 miles, the route extends from Happy Camp through BigFoot country to Willow Creek. The annual BigFoot Jamboree, held on Labor Day weekend in Happy Camp, celebrates the elusive, perhaps mythical Big Foot. Vendors, games, activities, and a parade bring hundreds of people to Happy Camp.

The Russian Wilderness Area is located along the major ridge that divides Scott and Salmon River watersheds. There are 22 lakes in the region, as well as a section of the Pacific Crest Trail.

Throughout the West, fires have become a dreaded, even terrifying reality. Each summer, as the winds blow across the timbered and brushy areas, fire becomes explosive. Unfortunately, while people in the old days burned the hillsides and mountainsides regularly—alleviating the danger of crown fires by removing dry and accumulating debris—people today fear fire. With the West becoming more and more like a tinderbox, the likelihood of continued and devastating forest fires increases dramatically. Already 2002 has been marred by dozens of crown fires.

Neither the Hog Fire of 1977 nor the Klamath Fires of 1987 began dramatically; both were sparked by dry lightning storms. But where homes were spared in the massive Hog Fire, the Klamath Fire destroyed many structures, including the historic Godfrey Ranch, a 160-acre homestead near Forks of Salmon. Others who lost homes included Mel Berry and Anne Pullen, Scott Morgan, Peter and Geba Brucker, Joel and Maryellen Stroge, Tim Darling, Wes and Grace Berry and their son Frank Berry, and Mel Berry's brother Walter. In the two months following the August 30 outbreak, fires swept through the mountains. The trees, according to Mel Berry, were little more than "smoldering sticks in the air." Another resident declared that the oncoming fire sounded "like 50 trains coming down the tracks at once."

Klamath River, Happy Camp, and Salmon River were literally submerged beneath a wall of darkness. City streetlights stayed on day and night. Temperatures began to drop because sunlight could not penetrate the heavy, ash-filled smoke. Trees began to go dormant while mushrooms, some growing several times larger than they usually grow, sprung up along the dark roadways. People with allergies and lung conditions were asked to leave the area. Others wore masks to keep the large particles of ash and debris from entering their lungs. Delegations from several countries, including Japan, even came to observe and take notes on what a "simulated nuclear winter" might be like.

Because of the towering plumes of smoke, coupled with the height of the Marble Mountains and the blustering winds, much of the heavier smoke was swept out of Scott Valley. Even with less smoke, the sun, when visible, shone through as a brilliant, deep red-gold. Scott Valley airport became a mini-city with blazing lights, helicopters, and other fire-fighting aircraft coming and going at all hours to transport men and equipment to the many fires. The tanker base in Montague dispatched borate planes whenever the winds shifted and visibility cleared enough for planes to fly safely.

The Annual Siskiyou County Balloon Faire went on as planned that year, coming only two weeks after the fires had begun, and was held in Scott Valley. While the local turnout was good, visibility was quite poor. And deer season, which normally begins the third weekend in September, had to be delayed for several weeks. Visibility was determined to be too poor to hunt safely.

After more than two months of battling nature and spending millions, the last of the fires were put out. Ironically, this was not achieved by man's efforts, but by the winter rains that arrived mid-November.

The 1987 Klamath Fire scorched 260,000 acres, making it the largest and the costliest in the history of the Klamath National Forest and northern California (up to that time). Of course, 2002 will become another record-breaking year in the West. According to records, the 1987 fire cost more than $80 million in suppression efforts and employed 10,000 people. Saddest of all was the loss of four firefighters. One, David Ross Erickson, 34, was from Etna. Part of a strike team, he was killed after being struck by a tree. Bruce Visser, 34, of Mountain Center, California, died when he was struck by a speeding motorcycle. Sergeant Donald Gormley, 47, of Eureka, California (of the California National Guard), was killed when he lost control of his vehicle while driving the winding road near Forks of Salmon. Freddie Pahnemah, 38, collapsed, and though a helicopter was dispatched, it was unable to land on the rugged stretch of mountain where Freddie was trapped. Tragically, the fires of 2002 have already taken more lives—14 at last count.

What made the Fire of 1987 unique, however, was that in order to log the remaining scorched or dying trees that stood along the steep slopes (partially burned trees are vulnerable to disease and decay), Cross and Kaufman, later renamed Crowman Corporation, expanded their use of helicopters. They were successfully able to remove single trees by lifting them out. But this was not without controversy. The environmental movement in California had other ideas. Injunctions and appeals started slowly. Certain timber parcels were targeted as sensitive areas. Then the list of sensitive sites grew until every potential timber sale in the Klamath National Forest was routinely protested. Even when issues were mitigated, protesters moved forward. Lawsuits were filed across the Northwest until a judge determined that lawsuits filed strictly for the purpose of delaying a sale without any factual basis would bring heavy penalties on those filing the suits.

The spotted owl also became a symbol representing endangered species throughout the Northwest. Unfortunately, scientists attached to the project expressed differing opinions about how to save the animal; if, in fact, it lived only in old growth forests; or whether it was even in danger of extinction.

Seeing their livelihoods shrink, loggers and those attached to the logging industry began to fight back. The 1980s and 1990s reflected this growing disharmony between the factions. An early organization constructed to limit or moderate wholesale restrictions placed on public timber lands was labeled the Win Back The West organization. This movement has since expanded to incorporate the concerns of such grassroots organizations as the Klamath Alliance for Resources and Environment (KARE) and Save Our Shasta and Scott Valleys and Towns (SOSS). These groups, made up of farmers, ranchers, loggers, educators, small business people, and others, have come together to promote the wise use of natural resources. KARE's first president in the early 1980s was Bill Overman. Other important individuals in its expansion, however, included Joan Smith of Montague and Carolyn Pimentel of Etna.

SOSS's origin is tied in directly with water issues facing farmers, ranchers, fishermen, and other local users. With the proposed listing of the Coho salmon as endangered, controversy over native habitat and boundaries, as well as what constitutes "good science," continues to rage. It is not an issue to be easily solved without participation by all factions. Other organizations, such as Siskiyou County Cattlewomen, the Cattlemen's Association, and Women in Timber are also working to moderate the conflict that exists within the county.

The upshot of the forest closures of the 1980s and 1990s was that private timber became a premium commodity. Even small parcels were bought up by logging companies. Timber prices jumped from $150 or $200 per thousand board feet (mbf) to $800 or $900 per thousand board feet. Mills around the Northwest, concerned that there would be no logs available if the court injunctions permanently halted timber sales on public lands, filled their mill yards to overflowing. Premiums were paid for each log. As a result, consumers paid triple the price. Finally, Canada began exporting lumber to the United States at much lower prices, forcing domestic prices to drop in order to remain competitive.

Most of the small logging operations and mills around Western Siskiyou County, however, could no longer stay in business. Others, like several Happy Camp mills, could not retool their mills to accommodate smaller sized trees being bought from private land sales. Most of these independent operators were forced to close, leaving sales traffic to push north into Canada. Communities in Western Siskiyou began to shrink, much as they had in the early part of the century when

SOAP CREEK FIRE. Firefighters marched to Hell Hole Lightning Fire Complex in 1927. (Courtesy U.S. Forest Service and Siskiyou County Museum.)

mining waned. As logging jobs disappeared, families with no other income moved to find work. Even today, school enrollment continues to decline and young families continue to leave as jobs still associated with timber are lost in the county's shifting economic tides. The major movement of population to the area involves retired people who have "made their money elsewhere" and come to experience the "slower pace of living."

The years following World War II brought natural disasters as well. In 1954 and 1955, a hard winter brought snow and rainfall that led to floods and hard conditions. Harold Slette of Fort Jones, then 22, said that as he and his future father-in-law Carl Mello fed Carl's cattle at Big Wheel Gulch on McAdams Creek Road in late December 1954, it rained hard. Even before they'd stepped out of the truck, they were soaked to the bone. When they finished their work, they looked down at McAdams Creek. The water was roaring.

> We saw a calf being carried down the creek. We couldn't get any wetter. We went in and drug the poor thing out. Good thing it was small or we couldn't have kept hold of it. They knew that the calf belonged to Bill Sorres, a neighbor who lived a mile further up the creek. They took the calf up and sure enough, it was Bill's. I don't know why that calf didn't

HELICOPTER LOGGING. *Logging a burned area, a helicopter hovers in the cold, snow, and fog. (Courtesy Jasha Reynolds Collection.)*

LITTLE NORTH FORK FIRE. A B-17 fire bomber drops fire retardant over a forest fire in the fall of 1969. (Courtesy U.S. Forest Service and Siskiyou County Museum.)

> drown. Bill had tough range cows and that must have had something to do with it. I don't know if the calf lived after all that but it was doing okay when we last saw it.

On December 18, 1964, torrential rain once more fell across Western Siskiyou County, making it nine years since the devastating floods of 1955. Warm rain melted the snow pack. Creeks overflowed and Scott River continued to rise.

In the middle of Scott Valley, Betty Young and her husband, Bob, went to tend the water, but "couldn't find the ditches; the water was so high it resembled a huge lake with trees growing up through the water." Betty remembers leaving her four daughters at home to go to Etna, but "the water was level with the highway [State Highway 3] across the bridge [at Patterson Creek]. We got as far as the Simmons house and looked back only to see a huge log rolling across the highway. We went back because we didn't want to be stranded." Later, they watched as the Patterson Creek Bridge nearly washed out.

When "Pinky" Bill Mathews and Ruthie, his daughter, pulled up with a load of Corrigan's horses, Bill got out and had Ruthie hold his legs, then he leaned over to look under the bridge. He said, "Hell, we can make it. It has six feet holding yet." So, he got into the truck, gave it the gas, and made it over. A county worker then dragged a long piece of metal siding across the road and said, "This may stop some other darn fool from trying to cross."

Water flowing over Scott River Bridge near Fort Jones was 18 inches deep. Mike and Don Eastlick launched a boat in the river to get a better look at the valley. The Fay Lane Bridge was out and *The San Francisco Chronicle* stated that "someone had seen quite a large salmon floating along the streets of Callahan."

The road between Etna and Callahan was nearly impassable. What had once been Highway 3 was now a narrow trail, a mere car width at most. Only the brave dared to take a car between the sheer bluff and the raging water. The approaches to the new Callahan Bridge across Scott River were washed out, while the old bridge remained intact and was quickly returned to use.

When the Patterson Creek Bridge washed out, the Siskiyou Telephone Company put in a footbridge. First, the phone company tried using a ladder truck to move people across the raging water. Bill and Danny Voight volunteered to try the "ladder route." Once the footbridge was completed, it was used constantly as

HOG FIRE. *This is a view of the burned area from Crapo Trail after the 1977 Hog Fire. (Courtesy U.S. Forest Service and Siskiyou County Museum.)*

HELICOPTER ASSIST. Firefighters fill portable, collapsible water bags that will be dumped on fires. (Courtesy U.S. Forest Service and Siskiyou County Museum.)

residents took care of their livestock and got groceries. Elizabeth Bigham, Tom Tickner, Tuffy and Connie Fowler, and others left their cars at Young's Ranch and had their families meet them at the footbridge.

On Christmas Day, it began to snow, and by January 5, there was a total of 30 inches on the Scott Valley floor. Sawyer's Bar reported 24 inches on the ground and there was over 12 inches in Happy Camp. Highways were closed 100 miles south of Siskiyou County.

Story has it that a small bird, displaced by the weather, took up residence in Eb Whipple's house for a bit of holiday cheer. The small, long-beaked creature enjoyed flying about the room, missing people by only inches. He seemed to consider Eb's Christmas tree his private palace and gave the ornaments quite a beating. He remained a slightly unwelcome, yet entertaining, visitor until the elements outdoors became more friendly and he returned to his flock with, no doubt, tales of his own.

John and Ida Larue, the Etna High School music teacher and Spanish teacher, respectively, were not daunted by the insanity of nature. They were married on December 31 in Etna and despite the difficulties, many attended the wedding.

On January 5, 1965, Betty Young wrote that this was "the strangest storm. It is raining and it is 30 degrees." On the January 7, there was a "beautiful red sky" and the temperature dropped to 10 degrees. That afternoon, another blizzard hit Western Siskiyou County. Bob Young led Dick Richmond's mules back to his house. Eb Whipple came over to help make roads and feed the cows.

Since the Etna Creek Bridge had been destroyed, Ariel Facey cut down a tree across Etna Creek so that the Siskiyou County Road Department could access its county yard south of Etna. The road department used power boats to check on residents of Scott Valley and assist in rescues when necessary, careful to maneuver around debris and fences hidden just under the surface of the water. Dick Smith and Paul Norris carried milk and bread from Fort Jones and through Thackeray's

CHARLES SNAPP. The longest-serving postal worker, Snapp was awarded a "stamp" in his image. (Courtesy Helen Lincoln Collection.)

fields to take to Etna families. The county tried to stop the erosion of the highway and bridge approaches in Callahan. Festus Facey ran a skiploader during the worst of the flood. He filled trucks with large rocks to dump where the road had once been.

Because the floods and subsequent snows had made most roads impassable, the road department went to the air. Harold Slette, who had only worked for the county since October of 1964, was one of the employees assigned to aerial surveys. "We flew in a helicopter over the Salmon River and lower Klamath trying to assess the damage. The water had taken out most of the bridges and culverts." When he wasn't in the air, Harold ran a Cat to help rebuild the bridge approaches in Callahan.

The Red Cross designated five citizens to purchase supplies and distribute them to Western Siskiyou residents. The five included Lloyd Coatney of Etna, Wilber Straits of Horse Creek, Mrs. Nellie Shomilin of Beaver Creek, Ernest Hayden of Callahan, and Tom Cloyd of Fort Jones.

A 12-dog dogsled from William E. Dog Sled Company of Orange County was brought in by Civil Defense. A mechanic had to get to the repeater station on Etna Mountain to fix a generator when the dogsled was called to assist in the rescue of Eva Roseberry, age 62, who lived 8 miles up Rattlesnake Creek, near Fort Jones. A 4-wheel-drive vehicle made it through 6 miles of snow, but it took the dogsled to complete the last 2 miles to the Roseberry cabin. Eva was taken by dogsled back to the waiting rig. It was thought she was the only person during the storm who had to be evacuated in this manner.

Twelve helicopters from the Air Force, manned by Vietnam veterans, were used in the evacuations. One pilot who flew a daring rescue was Bob Young from Alaska. He airlifted a young boy named Peter Prentice out of Salmon River. A pregnant woman, Ilea Fisher, was lifted out of Hamburg by a helicopter provided by the Bly Logging Company from Klamath Falls, Oregon.

Pilot Pat Patterson of the Western Helicopter Company of San Bernardino rescued an old miner named Andrew J. Barton. Patterson, Dr. G.P. Ashcraft, and USFS employee Bill Bathers landed near Forks of Salmon in Knownothing Canyon in a stream 3 feet deep. They then walked through 6 feet of snow for a quarter of a mile to reach Andrew's cabin. At one point, Dr. Ashcraft fell into a snow bank and went completely out of sight. When the rescue team arrived, they found Andrew suffering from double pneumonia, but he protested, "If my dog can't go out with me, I won't go." The small mongrel dog named Snookey got to go along for the ride. A ladder was dropped across the stream to get Andrew inside the helicopter. This time, Ashcraft fell into the water. The air temperature was around 10 degrees.

The trip home should have been easy, but Snookey was frightened by the loud noises of the helicopter and started to jump around. Ashcraft threw a leg over the dog to hold him down as they made their way to deliver medical supplies. Patterson says, "He [Ashcraft] was in those wet clothes for over two hours and he never complained once. He really worked hard and he's not a young fellow."

MIKE BRYAN AND FRIEND. Professional packer Mike Bryan takes a time out with one of his pack mule companions. (Courtesy Mike Bryan Family Collection.)

Another family who was rescued by helicopter was Francis Davis, his wife Grace, Francis Jr., and grandson Raymond Conrad Jr. (two years old). They had been stranded at their Ti Bar cabin by the Klamath River for ten days with only 15 pounds of potatoes, 3 pounds of shortening, 5 pounds of sugar, and a pound of coffee. Davis said later, "Nothin' was left when we were rescued."

The Carmichael home near Walker Creek had a hole knocked through the wall and debris was strewn about. California State highway bridges that washed out included Somes Bar, Orleans, Doolittle Creek, Swillup Creek, and Clear Creek. In all, 41 Siskiyou County bridges were taken out and 12 approaches were washed away. According to the road commissioner, A.A. Powers, "There may be more bridges out in areas which this department has not been able to reach." The roads that were declared washed out were as follows:

> In the Salmon River area—Crapo Creek, McNeal Creek, Somes Bar, Gibson Gulch, Taylor Greek, Little North Fork, Jackass Gulch, Blackbear, White's Gulch, Russian Creek, and three on Petersberg Road. In the Etna District—Sugar Creek, two on the South Fork, and four on French Creek. In the Scott River District—Shackleford Creek,

Meamber Creek, Middle Creek, Tompkins Creek, and one on the Serpa-Marlahan Road. In the Happy Camp District—Two on Elk Creek and three on Indian Creek.

The stores at Somes Bar and Forks of Salmon were inaccessible as a result of road-slides. One large slide was at Louis Creek, just above Somes Bar. The highway between Ti Bar and Clear Creek was also considered a total loss. Another slide took out 300 feet of the Scott River Road, and on the Salmon River, over 100 yards of highway a half-mile above Tripp Point was lost.

In addition to the private property lost, Etna's water and sewage system was severely damaged and the sewer and water system at Callahan Elementary were destroyed. Ed Burton of Quartz Valley was taken in by the Festus Facey family in Etna, along with all of his pack gear. When he returned home weeks later, he found that his house was still standing, but the flood waters had turned it 180

MIKE DEFARIA. In the 1980s, Mike was at work in a mill on the Salmon River. He also worked as a chrome and copper mining engineer during World War II. (Courtesy Jeff Buchin Collection.)

degrees and it was facing in the opposite direction. Other homes in Western Siskiyou were less damaged. The J.D. Proctor home was left on a high spot, though the flood took a room, storage shed, and most of the yard. Outside Callahan, Richard Hayden's house was sitting sideways on a cutbank that used to be Highway 3 and half of it was in the Scott River.

Siskiyou County turned out to be the hardest hit county inland, and Governor Edmund Brown issued a proclamation declaring a state of disaster for Siskiyou County. Representative Harold "Bizz" Johnson asked President Lyndon B. Johnson to declare Siskiyou County a federal disaster area.

The river gauges for the floodwaters of 1964 recorded readings that crested from 2 to 11 feet higher than comparative readings during the flood of 1955. Some of the rainfalls, as recorded by the USFS, were as follows:

GENERATIONS LATER. Dressed in traditional costume, young Amber Nichols wears a beaded, shell apron that has been passed down through the family. (Courtesy McBroom Family Collection.)

	Dec 1964	1955	normal	Jul-Dec 64	Jul-Dec 55
Callahan	14.63	11.84	3.56	18.59	9.05
Fort Jones	11.90	11.16	3.50	12.18	8.43
Sawyers Bar	25.84	20.77	10.00	35.28	21.33
Seiad	28.11	19.07	7.60	36.99	17.11
Happy Camp	30.39	25.05	9.68	42.71	24.03
Oak Knoll	17.71	9.30	4.09	23.60	9.22

Rainfall totals recorded in Wells History for the years:

	Nov	Dec	Jan	Annual rainfall
1861–1862	11.56	10.63	9.29	40.96★
1864–1865	6.00	12.75	1.87	26.77
1865–1866	9.79	1.21	6.59	35.65★★
1866–1867	2.51	11.75	9.12	28.38

★an unbroken annual rainfall record
★★including an unbroken March record rainfall of 9.02 in 1866

The first county estimates for damage ranged near the $3-million mark. The figures soon moved upwards when the waters began to recede. Over 200 buildings were damaged in Happy Camp, 50 were considered destroyed, and $5 million of damage was done to the Klamath area alone. The only fatality connected with the flood of 1964 was Paul Gillis of Tarzana, California. Paul, a member of the American Red Cross, was struck by a whirling helicopter blade at the Happy Camp Airport while unloading fuel.

The United States Army Engineers moved in and the first of 20 Bailey bridges, a portable bridge that could be disassembled (similar to an Erector set), was placed on Indian Creek, near Happy Camp, to open up Doolittle Road. Happy Camp was devastated by the combined flood waters of the Klamath River, Indian Creek, and Elk Creek. The homes of Agnes Warner and Paul Titus "floated away." The J.F. Sharp Lumber Company log deck of 4 million feet washed away and took out Indian Creek and a couple of old city bridges. The new concrete bridge on State Highway 96 was saved by the efforts of Tom Crocker Jr., who perched the 5-ton Carolina Plywood shovel crane on one end of the bridge and broke up the log jams created by the rogue logs from Sharps Mill. The Happy Camp Elementary School had 15 inches of water in the upper classrooms and 3 feet in the lower ones. The books were ruined and 4 feet of silt stood in the parking lot. Parts of town had mud and silt 10 feet thick.

This next is paraphrased and extracted from an eyewitness account by Mable Nitsch, in an article appearing in *The Siskiyou Daily News*: Somes Bar caught the brunt as the Klamath and Salmon Rivers combined. Wooley Creek bridge on the Salmon and Ishi Pishi bridge on the Klamath fell. Langford's store and post office and the Siskiyou Telephone toll phone also found a watery grave. Floyd Long, his son Glen, Melissa Langford, and her sister Ida Lake had taken supplies to Mrs.

Langford's home for safekeeping until the house started to slide down the mountain. Floyd lost everything when his home slid into the Klamath River. Melissa Langford lost two cabins and a wash house. Kenneth Sims of Ti Bar had remained in the building and was presumed drowned, but was later found sitting on a log that he had climbed on as his house floated away. USFS employees from Ti Bar moved to J. Epheriam's house on Ukonom Creek when their compound was washed away. When Payson Dietz and his wife Ethel were rushing away from the rising river, Ethel fell and broke her leg. They found refuge 2 miles away at Phil Bradley's.

Robert Nitsche and his father E.C. Nitsche put "a wire cable across the [Merrill] Creek for a highline and made a boatswain's chair." The next day, it got plenty of use when the culvert on Merril Creek washed out and left a 30-foot hole where the road had been. Thirty-four people were stranded and they had to use the highline to get to Long's for food.

It took several days for Red Cross to get through. The first evacuees, however, included Bessie Tripp; Vera Hastings; Mr. and Mrs. Leland Donahue and five children; Art Hickox; Mr. and Mrs. Joe Harrison and seven children; George Geary; and Mr. and Mrs. Joe Hechocota. All were transported to Yreka to stay with family and friends.

George Geary's home and belongings washed down the Salmon River. He did manage to save some bedding and Clancy Mills, his neighbor, saved his pickup truck, but Geary lost his trailer house when it was swept away with Joe Padil's house. Geary spent the night at Charlie Snapp's cabin, above the road, and Mills went to Oak Bottom Forest Service guard station with Steve Malone.

Statewide, there were at least 42 deaths, more than $700 million of damage done, and at least 4,775 homes destroyed. The Klamath carried its devastation, and that from Scott Valley and Salmon River areas, across Humboldt and Del Norte Counties out to the Pacific Ocean. Over 100,000 people in those two counties were cut off by flood waters. Truly, the floods of 1964 carried away more than debris and silt; for many people, it took away layers of their past. But as with every other kind of twist of fate, Western Siskiyou rallied its pioneer spirit and took to rebuilding the future.

The Backcountry Horsemen, a relatively new organization, came to Western Siskiyou ten years ago. The local chapter is known as Top of the State. It is a service organization that provides information and opportunities to improve recreation and tourism.

Members gather every few weeks to go on social and recreational rides. They combine a project or service with their fun. In the summer months, for example, they pack 5,000 to 6,000 fingerling brown trout and rainbow trout into the Marble Mountain Wilderness Primitive area in ice chests to lakes like Cliff and Campbell. These small fry are released into lakes inaccessible by air. The organization also maintains mountain trails and teaches the public how to use the forest responsibly. They also regularly compete in the county-wide Siskiyou Golden Fair with an informational booth.

EARLY DAY PACKERS. Pictured, from left to right, are (front row) F. Bradley, W. Balfrey, and P. Smith (blacksmith); (back row) B. Bradley, M. Isaacs, and J. Henderson. (Courtesy Hayden Family Collection.)

Most valley ranchers continue to pack into the mountains, even if it's only for a hunting trip between harvest and winter. Mike Bryan is a fourth-generation Scott Valley rancher who has turned his hobby into a profession. In 1987, he signed on to pack equipment and supplies into areas hit by the big fires. He now signs up for fire season each year in addition to taking recreationalists out into the wilderness and primitive areas. In 14 years, his business has grown, and the majority of his business now consists of repeat customers from the San Francisco Bay area. He says that things have changed in his lifetime and in the 50-some years he has taken friends, family, and customers into the mountains. "It used to be you were all alone on the trails except for a few other locals out fishing or on a pack trip or looking for their cattle. You knew everyone you met." After the Marble Mountains were designated a wilderness area in 1968, hikers, backpackers, and people trying to get out of the cities rushed to Western Siskiyou County.

In the 1980s, llama pack trains began keeping company with wary horses and mules in every meadow. In that same decade, elk were also reintroduced into the mountain areas. They have since thrived and can be seen all over Western Siskiyou County.

Dog racing is a passion for Pat Campbell of Callahan, who raises and cares for 42 dogs. A timber faller in the spring and summer, he spends his winters actively racing across the country. In 2002, after nine years of training and research, he was able to finish a race. He and his dog team placed 15th in the 350-mile Montana Iditarod-Race to the Sky. Maybe some day there will be a Callahan Iditarod.

Because the people who come to Western Siskiyou County have always been of an independent nature, it only seems fitting that Siskiyou should be at the forefront of a move to create a new state, not just in name or principle, but in reality as well. Its roots go back 150 years.

In 1852, a bill to create the State of Jefferson died in committee. On December 19, 1853, *The Daily Alta of California* of San Francisco suggested that northern California and southern Oregon could both benefit if a new state could be created. Some suggested it be called Klamath; others suggested the name Jackson. At a meeting held on January 7, 1854 in Jacksonville, Oregon, Lafayette F. Mosher spoke about a state of Jackson. Unfortunately, Mosher was the son-in-law of General Lane, who had well-known pro-slavery and anti–Native American beliefs, and the proposed state's identity was tainted by attitudes and unfounded fears.

In 1854 and 1855, the State Assembly tried to split California into three states: Shasta to the north, Colorado in the central part, and California to the south. But the Senate let the bill lapse. In 1877 and 1878, some again allowed "Shasta" and southern California to split, but the United States Congress declined.

By the fall of 1941, most communities were behind the idea. In a name contest, the State of Jefferson was officially born. Several counties joined in. Highways were blocked by guards armed with the declaration that the State of Jefferson would secede every Thursday until it became recognized as a state. The movement gained momentum until December 7, 1941, when secession took a backseat to the bombing of Pearl Harbor.

Even today, the dream lives on for this unrealized, some might say mystical, State of Jefferson. Here, baseball is still a favorite summer sport, along with fishing and hiking or packing into the Marble Mountain Wilderness. Occasionally, a large gold nugget is found. Deer, elk, bear, and raccoon are frequent visitors, as are Canadian geese and golden eagles. People work hard in order to sustain their lifestyles, however simple. The beauty of Western Siskiyou is still a source of pride, too often taken for granted. Ultimately, however, it cannot be destroyed by fire, flood, or man.

There is still no railroad through Scott Valley, but computers have connected Western Siskiyou with the world. Dairies and alfalfa flourish, and residents claim Siskiyou beef is the best. Wagons have given way to trucks. Riding is recreation and tractors do the work. There are even a few old miners squirreled up in hollowed canyons, while an Eastern Orthodox monastery and nunnery lay tucked away under the trees. And though wars have touched Western Siskiyou and taken far too many of the young, that old pioneer spirit prevails.

New adventures await the persistent. Naomi Lang, a member of the Karuk tribe, sought to fulfill her dream this year as she entered the 2002 Winter Olympics as the second Native American female to ever compete in an Olympic event and the first Native American female to compete in a Winter Olympics. Though Naomi did not win a medal or place in her skating events, her long-sought dream has inspired young Indians throughout Western Siskiyou County and the Northwest. Naomi and her skating partner Peter Tchernyshev did win four consecutive ice dance titles at the U.S. Figure Skating Championships, even scoring a perfect 6.0 in presentation (the third year they have scored 6.0 in national competition).

Western Siskiyou County may have indeed changed over the years, but in reality, what makes this region unique remains unchanged. Immortalized in metal, a packer and his pack horse, courtesy of Siskiyou County Poets, greet visitors as they approach Etna, a friendly reminder of days gone by.

ON THE TRAIL ONCE AGAIN. *This piece was created by Starritt of Yreka in honor of cowboys and packers in Western Siskiyou County. (Courtesy Gail Jenner Collection.)*

155

BIBLIOGRAPHY

Athearn, Robert G. *American Heritage Illustrated History of the United States*. Volume 13. New York: Choice Publishing, Inc., 1988.

Barrett, Carol. *As It Was: Stories From the History of Southern Oregon and Northern California*. Ashland: Jefferson Public Radio, 1998.

Bell, Maureen. "Hallie Daggett: Forest Guardian." *True West* (April 1994): 41-45.

Brewer, William H. *Up and Down California in 1860–1864*. Berkeley: University of California Press, 1966.

Campbell, Loreita M., ed. *Etna—From Mule Train to 'Copter*. Etna: Eschschotzia Parlor No. 112, Native Daughters of the Golden West, 1965.

Clark, William B. *Gold Districts of California (Bulletin 193)*. California Department of Conservation, Division of Mines and Geology, 1998.

Davies, Gilbert W. and Florice M. Frank. *Fort Jones (CA) 1853-1858: Military Notes*. Hat Creek: HiStory ink Books, 1994.

Davies, Gilbert W. and Florice M. Frank. *Thirty Country Road Loop Trips in Northern California*. Hat Creek: HiStory ink Books, 1995.

Davies, Gilbert W. and Florice M. Frank. *Memories from the Land of Siskiyou: Past Lives and Times in Siskiyou County*. Klamath Falls: HiStory ink Books, 1993.

Davis, Mary B., Editor. *Native Americans in the Twentieth Century: An Encyclopedia*. New York: Garland Publishing, Inc., 1994.

Green, Harry H. *Fort Jones Semi-Centenary*. New York: Office of Bronx Homes News, June 1921.

Hayden, Ernest A. *Along our History's Trail*. Callahan: Ernest A. Hayden, 1984.

Heizer, Robert F., ed. *George Gibbs' Journal of Reddick McKee's Expedition Through Northwest California in 1851*. Berkeley: Archeological Research Facility, Dept. of Anthropology, 1972.

Heizer, Robert F., ed. and William c. Sturtevant, gen. ed. *California (Vol. 8) of Handbook of North American Indians*. Washington, Smithsonian Institution, 1978.

Helsaple, Brian J. *Seiad Valley Tales and Tailings: Its Pioneers and the Yreka Gold Dredging Co*. Seiad Valley: Brian Helsaple, 1995.

Jones, J. Roy. *Saddle Bags in Siskiyou*. Yreka: News-Journal Printshop, 1953.

"Lotta Crabtree Lived in Yreka," *Yreka Journal*. (November 10, 1915).

McClain, Margaret S. *Bellboy: A Mule Train Journey*. Santa Fe: New Mexico Publishing Company, 1990.

Mortenson, Gary, ed. *September on Fire*. Fort Jones: Pioneer Press, 1987.

Parker, W.H. *Stockmen's Guide (Brands), Siskiyou County, California*. Etna: Balfrey Brothers, 1901.

Rock, James T. *The State of Jefferson: The Dream Lives On*. Yreka: Siskiyou County Museum, 1999.

Scott, Edwin. *California to Oregon by Trail, Steamboat, Stagecoach, and Train 1850 1887*. Pasadena: Pasadena City College, 1976.

Shaw, Elizur. *Emigrant Life on the Plains 1862*. Medford: Thomasine Swoape Smith, 1992.

Stumpf, Gary D. *Gold Mining in Siskiyou County 1850-1900*. Yreka: Siskiyou County Historical Society, Spring 1998.

Siskiyou County: A Time of Change. Yreka: Siskiyou County Historical Society, Spring 1976.

Siskiyou County Historical Society Yearbook, 1948. Yreka: Siskiyou County Historical Society, 1948.

Siskiyou Pioneer and Yearbook, The. Yreka: Siskiyou County Historical Society, 1950, 1957, 1960, 1961, 1963, 1964, 1966, 1978, 1982, 1983, 1990, 1994, 1996, 1998, 1999, 2001.

Terrell, John Upton. *American Indian Almanac*. New York: Barnes & Noble Books, 1971.

Tobie, Harvey E. "Stephen Hall Meek." *The Mountain Men*. (1949).

Todd, Lewis Paul and Merle Curti. *Rise of the American Nation*. New York: Harcourt Brace Jovanovich, Publishers, 1982.

Wells, Harry L. *History of Siskiyou County, California*. Oakland: D.J. Stewart & Co., 1881.

KARUK DIP NETTERS. Using traditional nets, these dip-fishers worked Ishi Pishi Falls c. 1900. (Courtesy Siskiyou County Museum.)

INDEX